POWER POINTS FOR MAXIMUM PERFORMANCE

Copyright © 2023 by Sam Chand

Published by AVAIL

All rights reserved. No portion of this book may be reproduced, stored in a retrieval system, or transmitted in any form or by any means—electronic, mechanical, photocopy, recording, scanning, or other—except for brief quotations in critical reviews or articles, without prior written permission of the author.

For foreign and subsidiary rights, contact the author.

Cover & interior design by: Joe De Leon of DeLeon Design
Cover photo by: Scott Rodgerson

ISBN: 978-1-960678-15-7   1 2 3 4 5 6 7 8 9 10

Printed in the United States of America

TURBO LEADERSHIP

POWER POINTS FOR MAXIMUM PERFORMANCE

CONTENTS

- **01.** Roles vs. Responsibilities 8
- **02.** Leading by Example 12
- **03.** Complex vs. Simple 16
- **04.** Great Opportunities 20
- **05.** Connecting Vision to People 24
- **06.** Discovering Potential Leaders 30
- **07.** Honesty in Leadership 34
- **08.** Information and Inspiration 38
- **09.** Keeping Your Focus 42
- **10.** Changing Your Mind 48
- **11.** Admitting Mistakes 52
- **12.** Helping Others 58
- **13.** Gaining Credibility 62
- **14.** The Need for Respect 66
- **15.** Handling Criticism 70
- **16.** Solutions 74
- **17.** The First Step 78
- **18.** Eloquent Listening 82
- **19.** Generating New Thoughts 86
- **20.** Change 92

21.	Learning From Disappointments	98
22.	Dealing With Underperformance	104
23.	Sustaining Momentum	108
24.	What Is and What If	114
25.	Thinking New	120
26.	Intent vs. Impact	124
27.	When Your Vision is Greater Than Your Resources	128
28.	Your Style of Leadership	132
29.	Internal Conflict	138
30.	Safe Zone to Brave Zone	144
31.	Getting Unstuck	150
32.	What's Important	156
33.	Leading Where You Haven't Been	160
34.	Forgiving and Moving On	164
35.	Selling Your Idea	170
36.	Decision-Making vs. Implementation	174
37.	The Journey	178
38.	Purpose and People	184
39.	Choice-Rich	190
40.	My Greatest Regret	194

TURBO LEADERSHIP | POWER POINT ONE

ROLES VS. RESPONSIBILITIES

8

LEADERSHIP IS NOT A ROLE. IT IS NOT SOMETHING YOU DO. IT'S A RESPONSIBILITY RELATED TO WHO YOU ARE.

Leadership is not a role. It is not something you do. It's a responsibility related to who you are. Often, when I'm working with leaders, I will ask them, "What are you?"

Let's use an example answer. Let's say they tell me, "I am a CFO."

That's a role. However, that's not the answer I'm interested in primarily. I am interested in your level of *responsibility*.

This CFO might continue by telling me, "Well, I manage this budget, this team, this meeting, and these other items on a weekly and monthly basis."

Unfortunately, that's still not how a CFO should be defined. Your responsibility, at its simplest, is to keep the organization fiscally healthy. That's the bottom line, your ultimate answer to the question, "What is your job?"

How you carry out that responsibility—how you organize your team, how you manage the people that you have on it, how you utilize software or implement processes—is wonderful to know and to systematize in order to train up others, but those details don't constitute your responsibility. They're just the specifics that support it. It's essential for us to look beyond the day-to-day details and define what our lasting impact is; otherwise—if we don't know what we do—no one else will be able to discern it, either.

Again, your primary responsibility as a CFO is to keep the organization financially healthy. If you truly want to make a lasting difference—if you want to look back in ten, twenty, or thirty years and marvel at the potential you maximized—it's imperative that your perspective is bigger than the details. Each day, don't ask yourself, *What's my role?* This makes it too easy to get bogged down in minutiae and miss opportunities for true influence. Instead, inquire of yourself daily, *What's my responsibility?* How do you answer that question? How do you know what your responsibility is? How do you differentiate between it and your role, no matter your position?

In case you're still stumped as to what your responsibility is, here is the most helpful question: If you were to stop doing what you do for the next two months, *what would fall apart*? In the case of our CFO, the company would no longer be able to remain financially healthy. Yes, there are many specific answers to that question, but the overarching one makes the responsibility clear.

> **IF YOU WERE TO STOP DOING WHAT YOU DO FOR THE NEXT TWO MONTHS, WHAT WOULD FALL APART?**

Look at your responsibility. What would fall apart if you weren't there to take care of it? Whatever your answer is reveals your responsibility. The other items—the things that *will not* fall apart—will work themselves out.

Ask yourself that question. Don't be scared by the answers, and don't simply put a plan in place without truly understanding the nature of what you do. As a leader, it's not your role that is most pivotal; rather, it is your responsibility that you most need to prioritize.

POWER POINT TWO

2 LEADING BY EXAMPLE

TURBO LEADERSHIP

12

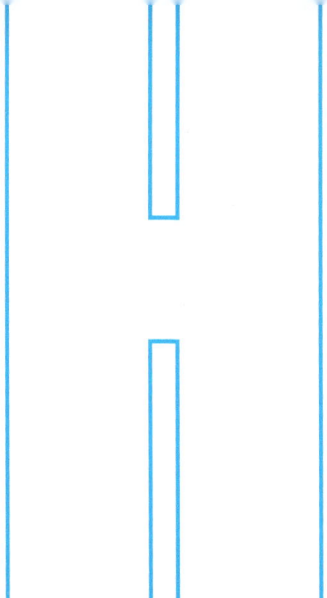

Have you heard the old adage, "Do as I say, not as I do"? It might sound inspiring, but in the end, we've seen that it doesn't work very well, does it? Think about it: People don't do what you do. People do what they *see* you doing. I have found this to be true in my life—in the places I consult, with the people I assist and the leaders I talk to every day, and on the stages where I speak.

Picture this: There is a camera on you all the time. It doesn't matter where you go—it is watching everything about you. It sees you when you're nice and when you're rude. The lens captures you when you give somebody time or you cut someone off on the way to work. Whether you are generous with your resources or stingy with what you have, make room for others or squeeze others out, give credit or hoard credit—at all times—its focus is trained on you.

Who or what *is* this hypothetical camera? The camera is all the people you are leading. They see more than you think they see. People are more observant of you than you realize! The pivotal question is this: If everybody acted according to how they saw you acting, what kind of organization would you have? Be brutal with yourself when you answer this question because it's true: Everybody is watching you. That is why it's vital to lead by example.

Think about the people you've learned from—the leaders who have influenced your life. Maybe they were mentors, parents, teachers, coaches, professors, or businesspeople. It's not what they told you that has most shaped who you are today, although we often remember key principles taught to us by those we respect. Rather, it's their lifestyles—their powerful examples—that we most admire, remember, and often emulate. The same is true today of you and those who are looking up to you. It's not enough to say the right things; the odds are that empty words won't stick with them for years to come. You have to live out the example you hope to pass on to them.

Being on time is a great illustration. Would you walk into a meeting late and expect everyone else to be there on time (unless you're the king)? People notice when you're not on time. They see

PEOPLE DON'T DO WHAT YOU DO.
PEOPLE DO WHAT THEY SEE YOU DOING.

the traits and qualities you put on display—even when you're not thinking about them.

So what are people seeing when they see you? That's an important question . . . an introspective question. Once you embrace that people will mimic behavior, not speech, you can begin to be more self-aware and act according to your values and principles, as well as the vision of your organization.

POWER POINT THREE

03
COMPLEX VS. SIMPLE

TURBO LEADERSHIP

16

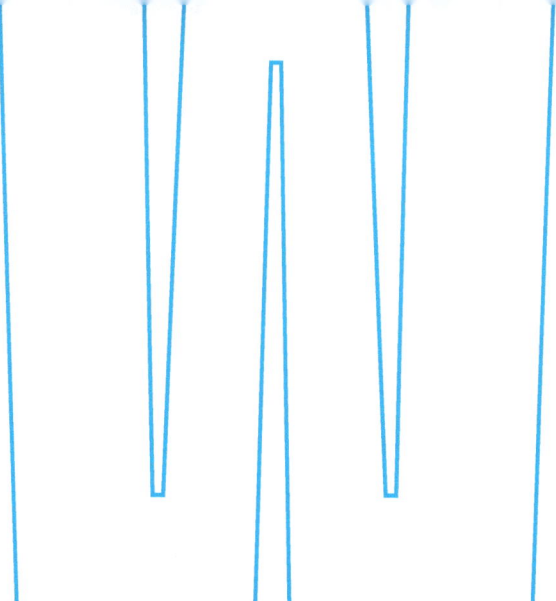

We're living in a world where everybody gets jazzed by complexity, but if we're honest, nobody's impressed with it. My philosophy is that it's better to keep things simple.

My wife bought one of those fancy toaster oven/air fryer/convection appliances—the kind of gadget that performs all the miracles a chef could imagine. When I opened the box, I found two manuals that came with the product. One was basic. It held instructions along the lines of, "Open it up. Do this to make French fries. Do this to make toast. Do this to broil. Do this to bake." This first manual contained pictures and straightforward instructions, numbered one through five, that streamlined the process of setting the device up and cooking the food.

The other manual was the size of a book and contained information about all kinds of intricate operations. You could cook and create food in a multitude of ways with this device. It looked like it would take weeks just to wade through the number of steps and wealth of information contained in its pages. You can guess which manual I felt inclined to start with in my quest to set up the appliance, can't you?

This object lesson comes back to me now as I consider the dichotomy of complexity versus simplicity. Do you know what gets the job done most quickly? Putting away the complex book of instructions and looking first at the simple pamphlet. When we begin working through the elementary instructions, we see immediate results, and we don't get bogged down in the details. Complexity might be impressive, but simplicity gets things moving.

Maybe you've seen this in your own role at your organization. There are a million details and instructions that could fill your meetings, your inbox, your mind, and your schedule. Often, these are what dominate your waking hours, leaving you frazzled, stressed out, and feeling as if you're in a lifelong game of Whac-A-Mole. It's not that these details aren't important—especially if you need to reference a more specific strategy or source of information. But why do we so often start by overwhelming ourselves with more than we need? Our default should be, instead,

COMPLEXITY MIGHT BE IMPRESSIVE, BUT SIMPLICITY GETS THINGS MOVING.

to begin simply and add as we go if and when we need to add. If we take this principle to heart, we'll find our minds calmer, our vision clearer, and our calendars streamlined to handle the things that will truly make a difference.

The next time you're going into a meeting, ask yourself how you can streamline the elaborate. Good leaders can take the difficult and make it easy. Simplifying things is harder than complicating them. As leaders, we have a love affair with having "one more point," "one more layer," or "one more box." The hardest work you're going to do as a leader is to take something complicated and make it plain. Simplify your role and the elements of it, and you will achieve the complex.

POWER POINT FOUR

4 GREAT OPPORTUNITIES

TURBO LEADERSHIP

20

GREAT OPPORTUNITIES

As a leader and as a human being, I have learned to appreciate being told no. Our human nature is to balk when someone denies our requests, but let me explain why it's healthy and even beneficial to hear this dreaded two-letter word.

The reality is that we've all been told no at some point in our lives. Conversely, we've told others no. When it comes down to it, life is *full* of nos. So why shouldn't we be depressed about it? Because beyond our initial reaction to being told no is the opportunity to discover something even better than the closed door in front of us. When you are told no, maybe you experience deep disappointment or pain. Anger, resentment, a loss of hope, or any number of negative feelings are healthy and normal. After all, some of us have been denied dreams, relationships, connections, opportunities, or other tangibles we've worked hard for and yearned to take hold of for a long time. It's okay to mourn those things.

And, as I take inventory and look back on my life, I see the flip side of no. I see that my greatest opportunities came precisely because somebody first told me no. I grew in the "no" moments of life and developed a bigger perspective to see outside the singular situation I had been so fixated on previously. I was only able to relocate to the site of my next opportunity because I could not find someone to sell me a house. Looking back, if I had bought a house in my old locale, I would not have been able to seize that next open door. However, somebody said no, and I did. I have also found that every no is pregnant with a yes. Every no has possibilities inside of it.

So, look at your life. Think about it for a moment. Consider all the memories, transitions, lessons, and difficult circumstances you've survived thus far. Think of all the major places where you have heard someone say, "No, you may not do that. No, you can't have that job. No, no, no." As you look back on those memories, ask yourself, *What came out of those nos?* Perhaps some of your greatest opportunities came from being told no, redirecting your course, or considering other options after encountering closed

I GREW IN THE "NO" MOMENTS OF LIFE.

doors. The greatest possibilities arose for so many people we admire in the middle of their nos.

Every no is pregnant with a yes. So, feel the pain. Feel the disappointment. Feel your feelings because they are human, and they are healthy. Feel them all, but don't let them hold you back in the long run. Hear that no, process it, and then look around and assess the opportunities that are still in front of you. A simple no can open doors you never thought possible! Appreciate the power of no! And while you're at it, don't be afraid to say no to things and to people when necessary!

05
CONNECTING VISION TO PEOPLE

POWER POINT FIVE

TURBO LEADERSHIP

24

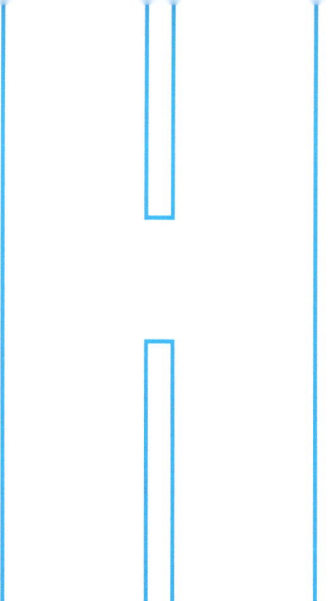

How do you connect your people to your vision? This is a concept essential for anyone in a leadership role to grasp—whether you're the primary leader, a departmental leader, or a volunteer leader, it really doesn't matter. You have to know how to connect your people to your vision.

First, you need to understand what your vision is and what it's not. Your vision is not a speech, a bunch of PowerPoint presentations, a document, or a compilation of information and data.

Your vision *is* your heart. So, rather than merely telling people the vision, we take a journey with the vision and invite them to come along. We inspire them along the way. We invigorate them for their own excursion. We ask them questions about their visions and how they tie into the bigger picture you're pursuing together. When was the last time you sat down with your team and asked them questions that revealed their hearts and shed light on the paths they've taken? Do you know what drives, inspires, and motivates them? What makes them angry, keeps them up at night, or gets them up in the morning? It may seem irrelevant to know these details, but it couldn't be more important to realizing the vision of your organization.

What are we trying to do? We're trying to find different creeks and tributaries with which to create the big river. This is what is known as confluence. Confluence asks the simple question, "How many smaller rivers are flowing into this mighty big river?" That's what vision is about. It is about their lives flowing into your life and how you can realize the vision together. The truth is that you'll never realize your vision by yourself. Vision is a communal thing—it takes support, advice, and teamwork to realize it.

Many leaders get caught up in vision-casting as a solo endeavor—trying to capture vision all by themselves and transmit it without accepting anyone else's feedback. But as I said earlier, vision is not an announcement you make in a keynote speech. Instead, it is an invitation to take the journey together. You bring

YOUR VISION IS YOUR HEART.

together their journeys, your journey, and the organization's journey in order to find commonality and move your purpose forward.

Yes, this is more difficult than simply broadcasting your own idea of what needs to happen; that's why leadership, on any level, is a significant responsibility. You're not just dictating—you're fostering others' potential, stewarding their stories, and cherishing their contributions.

How do you invite people into this excursion called vision? Instead of merely telling them what to do, you genuinely invite their journeys to have confluence with yours. This takes selflessness, respect, and maturity—all traits of a great leader.

So, what motivates your team? What are their unique visions, and how do they align with the vision of your organization?

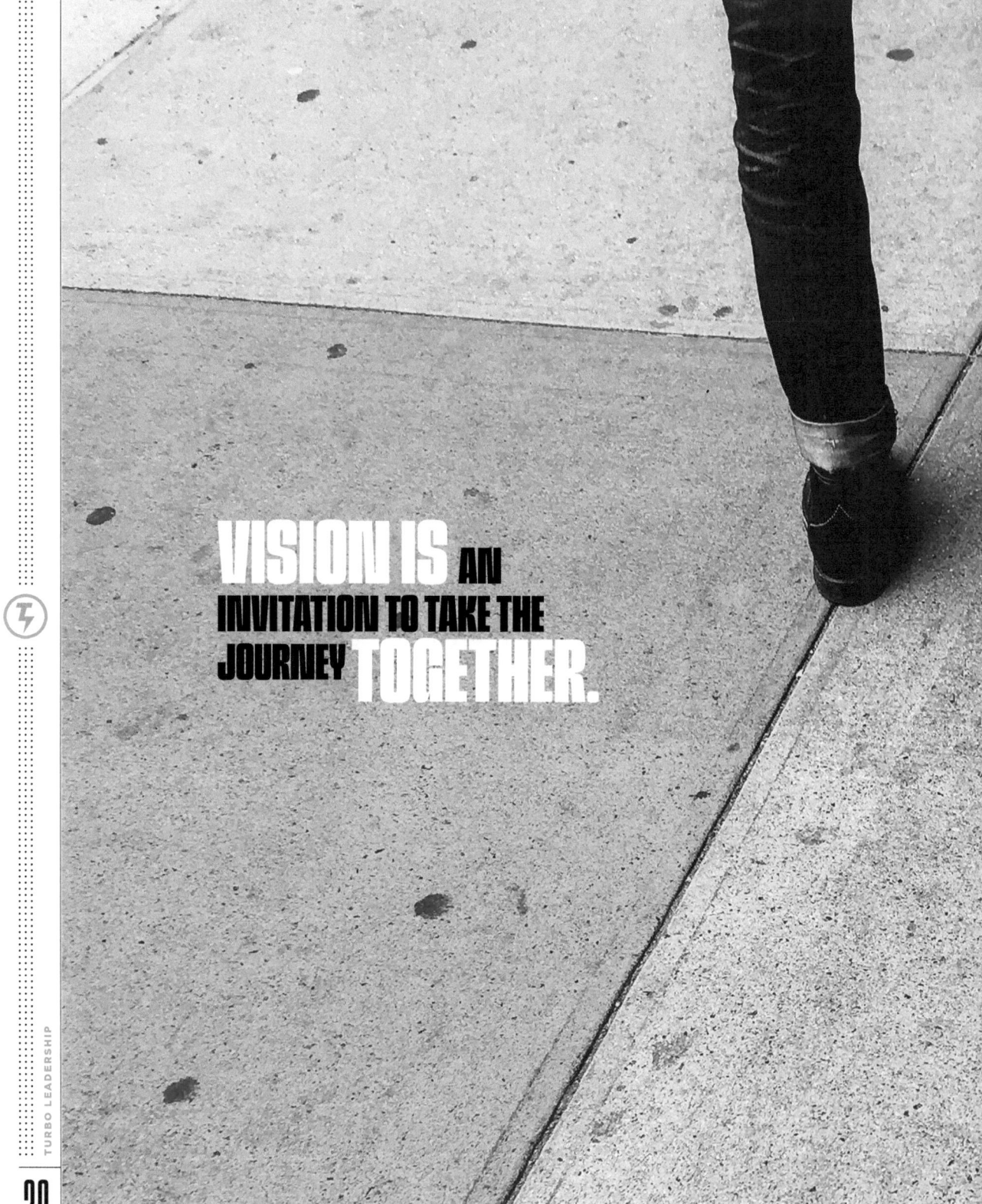

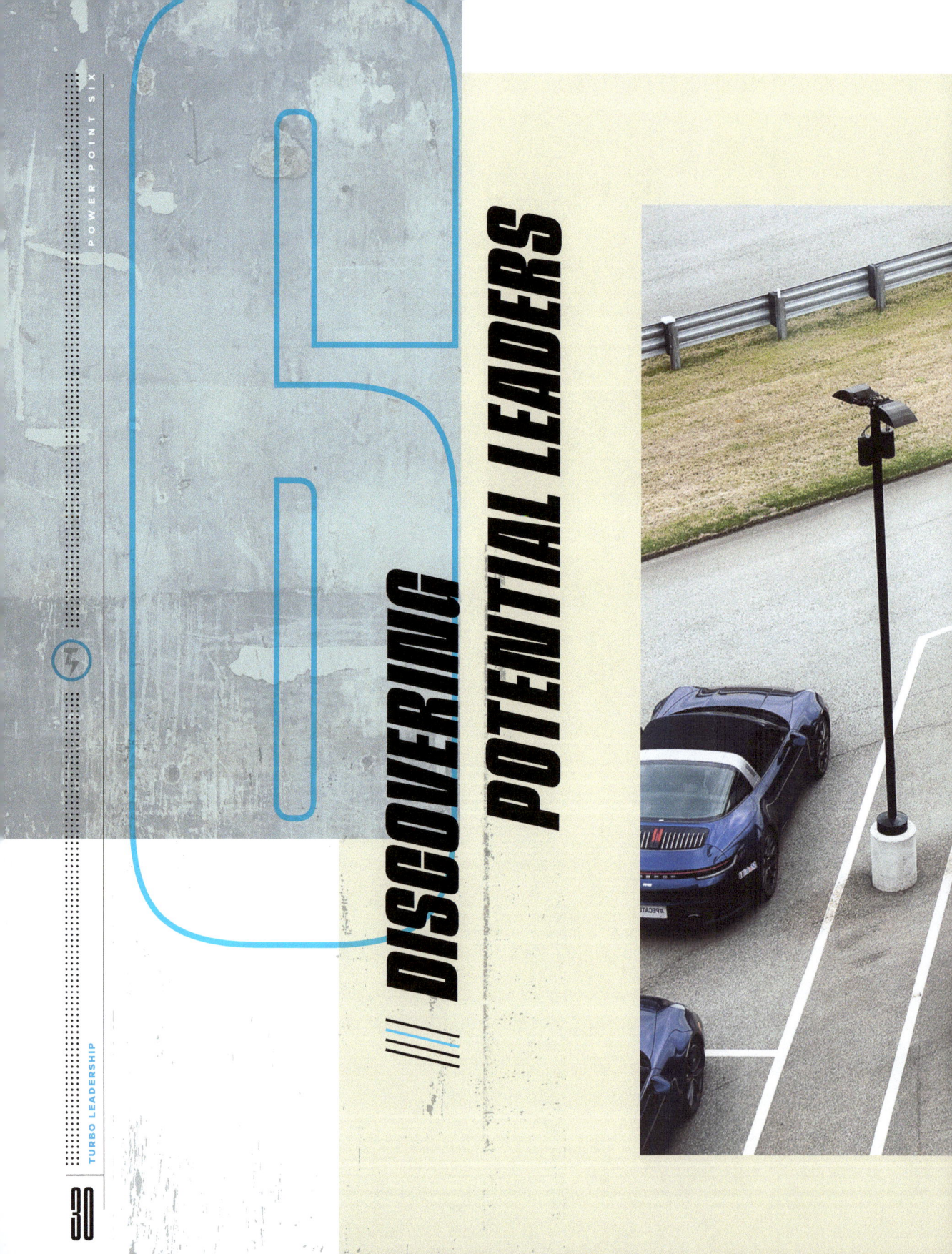

POWER POINT SIX

06

// DISCOVERING
POTENTIAL LEADERS

TURBO LEADERSHIP

30

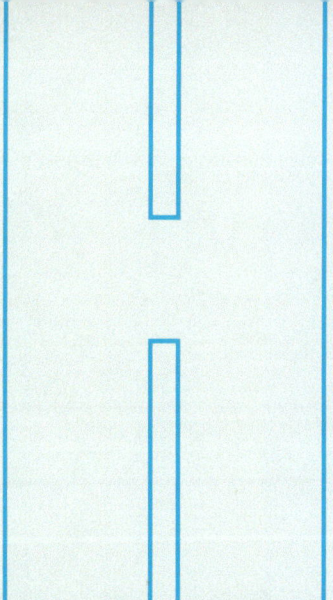

How do you discover potential leaders? Let me clarify what I mean by this question. I don't mean polished leaders... or perfect leaders... or even experienced leaders. I'm interested in how you discover *potential* leaders. After all, part of our job as leaders is to steward and foster others' potential so that they grow into the best versions of themselves, right? So, what am I looking for in budding leaders?

Here's an example of how I think about this. I had a gentleman reach out to my office and ask if he could speak with me for a few minutes. I didn't recognize him from anywhere, and I wasn't sure how he knew me. We gave him a time and a date, and I got on the phone with him. We ended up having a good conversation—one that I didn't want to end. Why was this talk so compelling?

He was a thirty-two-year-old young man. I had never met him before; however, when I hung up from that phone call, I thought to myself, *If I were hiring, I would hire him*. Keep in mind that I had not given this person any personality or leadership assessments to take. I had not shaken his hand. I hadn't gotten to see him face to face. I hadn't heard about his employment history or his top skills. I didn't know anything about him except what I learned while talking to him for five minutes.

Do you know why I would have hired him? Here are a few reasons: He was curious and authentic. He had more questions than answers yet more solutions than problems. He thought about the "what if" scenarios. He was actually interested in my life, not just interested in me talking to him. All of these things created a mental picture for me that told me he had amazing potential.

So, how do you look for amazing potential? Look for the people who are curious. Look for the people who get it—you cannot measure that skill. It won't show up on assessments, but the people who get it have immeasurable potential. Look for the people who have good questions because good questions lead to great answers. It's the level of questions people ask that get them to where they are in life.

Look for people who have options—not this or that but this *and* that. Look for people who see possibilities and say, "I don't know, but I can find out." Look for people with admirable work ethics. Look for people hungry to learn, grow, absorb information, and serve others at the expense of their own comfort. Look for the raw potential in people. That is how you discover potential leaders! Do not look for the finished product; look for the raw materials.

After all, someone saw the raw potential in you and took the time and effort to help develop it!

> **IT'S THE LEVEL OF QUESTIONS PEOPLE ASK THAT GET THEM TO WHERE THEY ARE IN LIFE.**

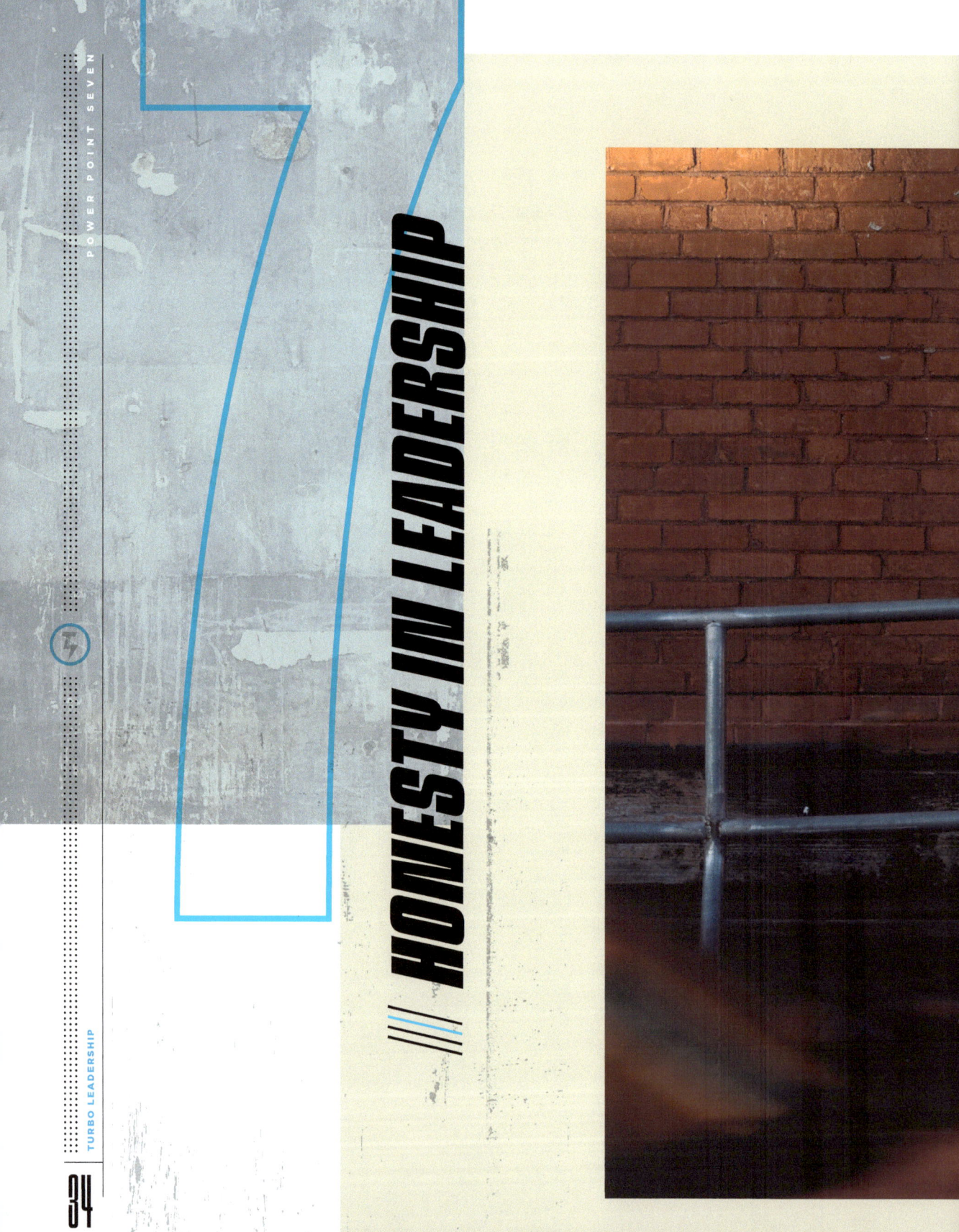

7

POWER POINT SEVEN

HONESTY IN LEADERSHIP

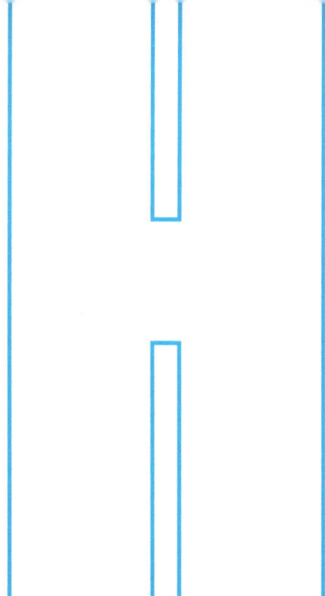

Here's an unpleasant truth: People have unrealistic expectations of you as a leader. They want you to always be smiling and happy, to always have solutions and everything under control. Is this realistic? Of course not. But it's reality for many of the people you lead.

Most people have totally impractical preconceptions regarding where the organization ought to be, how you should be treating them, what their roles should be, what they should be paid, what promotions they should be getting . . . and the list goes on and on. These oversimplified expectancies are present in most organizations around the world. Unfortunately, this results in part from the way we have allowed people to view us.

Think about the immense pressure we as leaders put on ourselves to maintain a certain image. We assume that the ideal perception for others to have of us is a faultless, ever-energetic leader whose vision is above reproach or correction. We've seen how this false self-image plays out in unhealthy leaders in every sphere of influence around the world; nobody buys it. We each know that we're fallible—and we definitely know that our leaders are fallible. We actually do ourselves a disservice by pretending to be something we're not, and we foster those unrealistic expectations that weigh us down consistently.

I have a bold suggestion: Just be honest with your team. Be vulnerable with them. They'll respect you more for your authenticity. Allow time for them to ask you the hard questions. Don't put a spin on things. The more spins you put into motion now, the more you'll have to stop later because they have a way of gaining momentum on their own. Tell them about the days you have a hard time. Share with them the things you want to improve upon—the areas in which you want to grow in the upcoming months. It may seem backward, but this will actually garner you more respect from those you lead than pretending you have it all together.

What I'm suggesting to you is vulnerability. This will often involve saying things such as, "I don't know," "Let's all find out," "Let me pray about it," "Let me get back to you about it," "I've never been down this road before," and "That's a great question—can we talk about that?" It is being honest with your people. I guarantee that you'll be happy with the results. When you're honest with your people, your authenticity, genuineness, and integrity will rise to a higher level with them, and they will know you are a truth-teller. They'll take you at your word because you'll have shown them that you see them as equals.

They will come to trust that you're not trying to manipulate the facts, so you come off in a better light. You won't be trying to keep information from them any longer, and because of that, your leadership equity will rise.

> **WHEN YOU'RE HONEST WITH YOUR PEOPLE, YOUR AUTHENTICITY, GENUINENESS, AND INTEGRITY WILL RISE TO A HIGHER LEVEL WITH THEM, AND THEY WILL KNOW YOU ARE A TRUTH-TELLER.**

At first glance, it seems as if information and inspiration are at opposite ends of the spectrum. In reality, while there is a difference between those two words, the truth is that each of us needs both in order to lead effectively. You can have all the information you want, in any format—data, PowerPoints, spreadsheets, videos, presentations, and more—but having all of that information does not automatically translate to success for your team. Information alone is not motivating for people.

Think about the times in your journey in which you've been equipped with head knowledge. Maybe you had a job training, educational course, or another source of information. Just being given that knowledge didn't automatically stoke your motivation and passion for that area of expertise, did it? Maybe your job was in an arena you really didn't care about, or your parents pressured you to get a college degree in a major that was different from your desired course of study. These are prime examples of the truth that information—in and of itself—doesn't motivate people. It's a good foundation, but in order to be influential, it needs inspiration to accompany it.

Inspiration is what people feel; information is how they think. You need both of these because information without inspiration is dry and has no meaning to it. Conversely, if you have only inspiration and no information, there is nothing tangible to hold onto when the going gets difficult. You'll be fired up in the good times and discouraged quickly when things turn for the worse. If, however, you are willing to provide both data and motivation to those you lead, you can give them a powerful opportunity to be successful in their goals and effective in their influence. Remind yourself that you must inform *and* inspire your team. In doing this, you're bringing two very strong components together that can bond and move your organization forward.

So, which part should you focus on providing more of to your team? Well, every leader already has information. You have data. You have people who provide you with reports and analyses regarding what you want to do in the future. Your role, your specific offering, is inspiration. So when you're preparing for your next meeting, ask yourself, *How can I spur my people to act on the information that we have?* You may have to get creative or innovate. You may have to generate enthusiasm within yourself before you're able to bring it out in others. This is a worthwhile investment, though, both for you and for those you inspire. So take the time and put in the work to ensure that your team is passionate about what you're doing together.

If you spend more time figuring out how to stimulate your team, you will see instantaneous results. You will always have information, but you won't always have inspiration. Integrate both into your leadership, and you will keep going higher and higher.

> **HOW CAN I SPUR MY PEOPLE TO ACT ON THE INFORMATION THAT WE HAVE?**

POWER POINT NINE

KEEPING YOUR FOCUS

TURBO LEADERSHIP

42

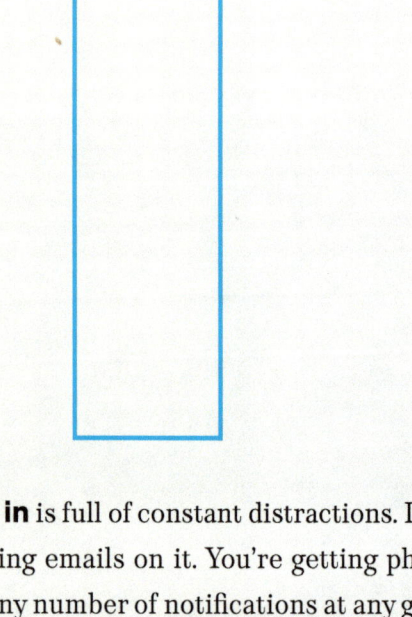

The world we live in is full of constant distractions. If you have a phone, you're getting emails on it. You're getting phone calls, text messages, and any number of notifications at any given time. You have Facebook on it, and/or Twitter, Instagram, LinkedIn, and the list goes on and on. My point is that the little gadget in your pocket is going *ding, ding, ding*—distraction, distraction, distraction—all the time.

This rings true (pun intended!) even outside of our phones. As a leader, you might have a separate place where you check email or other notifications, like an online work portal. You may have an office phone. You have customers or clients who walk into your office or physical mail that gets delivered. If your office has a television, it's also deluging you with stimulation and information. Have you ever played the radio at work? There's another source of noise. We're absolutely inundated with content, and it leaves very little time for conscious, focused thought—let alone focused action.

My guess is that you know someone—whether it's a friend or a coworker—who loves to brag about how good they are at multi-tasking. However, this simply isn't a skill that human beings thrive in! We physically cannot excel at tasks when we're distracted by other stimuli. I have a question for you: If your surgeon is doing

TURBO LEADERSHIP

46

surgery on you, do you want *them* to be multitasking? How about the pilot of the airplane on which you are flying? Or do you want them to be focused? As a leader, you can ask yourself this question on a daily basis: *Am I multitasking, or am I focused? Am I an attentive leader, or am I preoccupied?*

So what exactly happens to our minds and our bodies when we multitask? What most people don't understand is that every time you go from one task to another (to another, to another, to another), shifts are taking place in your brain. Segues are being created. Transitions are taking place, and you're moving from one zone to the next. The trouble with this is that each unique zone calls for a different kind of thinking. For example, if I'm studying biology, mathematics, and physics all at the same time, they may seem similar on the surface, but each subject calls for information and energy from a distinctly different portion of my brain. This is why we are most effective when we buckle down and truly hone in on one thing at a time. Our minds retain information more easily, we feel less stressed, and we're able to maximize our time and energy. Isn't that what leadership is all about?

> **WE ARE MOST EFFECTIVE WHEN WE BUCKLE DOWN AND TRULY HONE IN ON ONE THING AT A TIME.**

As a leader, how focused are you? Is that little thing in your pocket, or all the people around you, or the knock on the door, or all of your multitasking taking you away from your ultimate focus? Be a surgeon. Concentrate.

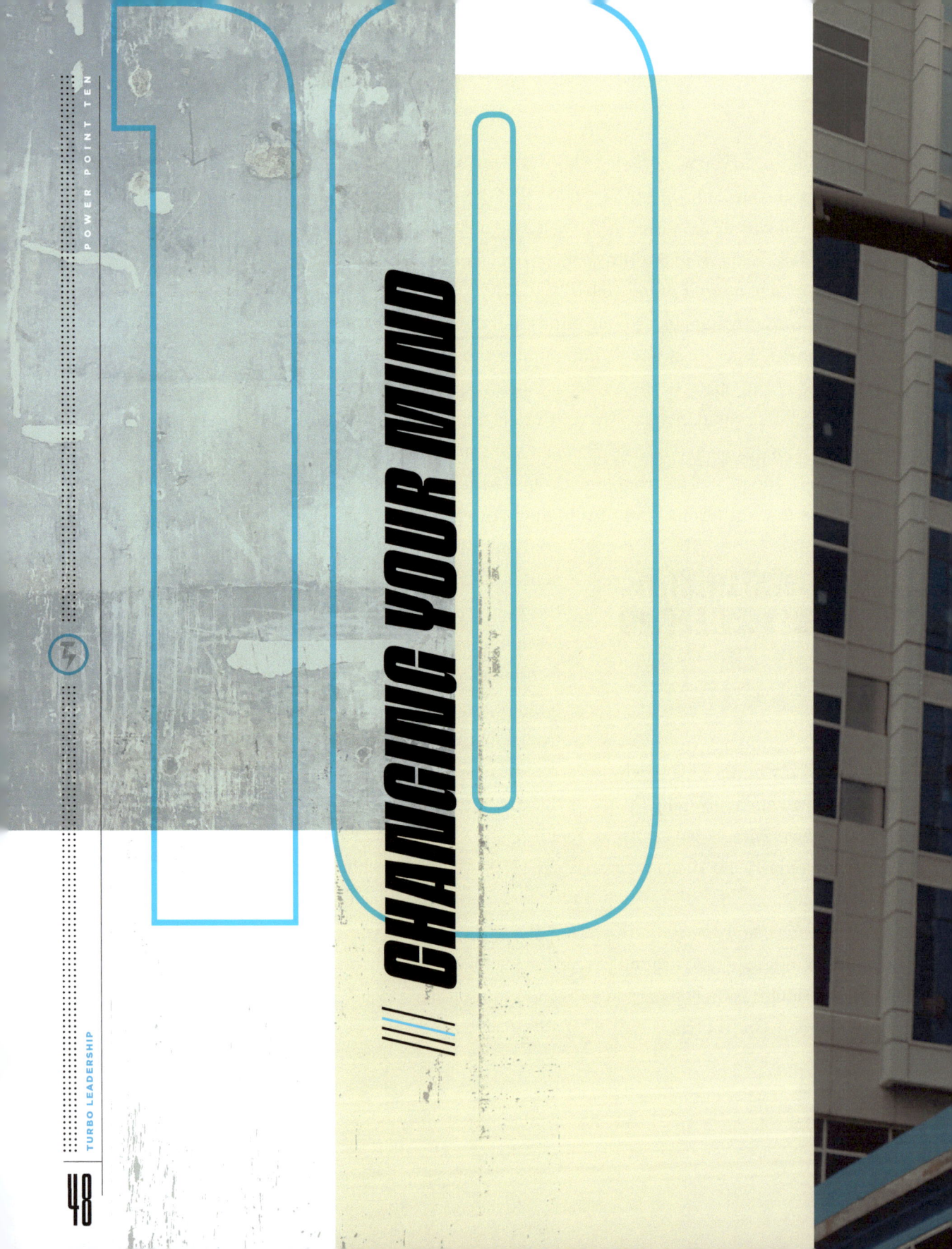

CHANGING YOUR MIND

49

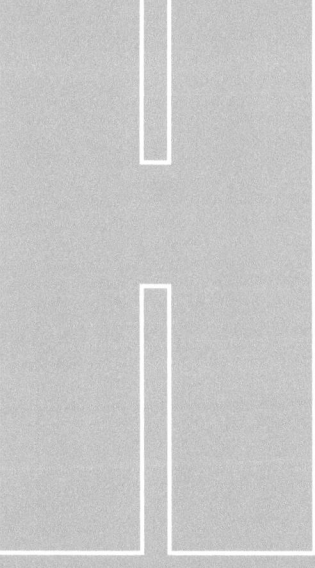

How difficult is it for you to change your mind?

I personally have a hard time doing this. Maybe that's true for you, as well. Changing our minds is difficult for the majority of us because we form opinions, and then we calcify them. This is the hardening process in which we subconsciously decide that we are not going to change our opinion. Everything becomes so arthritic, at times, that we have a hard time changing our minds, even when it's beneficial for us to do so. We've all met someone who refuses to change their mind, even in the face of clear evidence to the contrary.

Here's what I've learned: The most important change a person will ever make is in changing his or her mind. There are an infinite number of areas and opportunities in which you can do this. You can change your mind about what church means to you, what your company means to you, what you think when someone messes up when they have been good before, whom you do business with, and how you manage your finances, your family, or your team. You can have second thoughts about what you like, what you're pursuing, the goals you have for this season, who you want to do life with, and so many other things. You change your mind about

THE MOST IMPORTANT CHANGE A PERSON WILL EVER MAKE IS IN CHANGING HIS OR HER MIND.

many different things each day without realizing it; these changes are significant because they alter our paths.

The challenge is taking your mind into places that you don't want to go—changing the opinions that you'd rather not face. Most people don't want to go there because they know that changing *those* opinions means having to put aside a beloved old way of thinking in order to take on something new and uncomfortable. And let's be honest: it's human nature to stick to what we know and what has worked for us in the past!

Our minds have a way of forming opinions, setting in stone, and never letting go of them. But if you do the work to change your mind based on new information and experience, it'll be the best change you can make. You'll find that you're more receptive to those you lead, able to connect more easily with the next generation, capable to keep growing as a person—no matter your age—and quicker to catch on to new and effective strategies.

So the question to ask yourself today is this: *What am I going to do when I have an opportunity to change my mind?* When you encounter that new information or have that new experience, are you going to resist it, argue with the facts, or push back against the people trying to benefit you by teaching you? Or are you going to listen and embrace a humble spirit? The opportunity to change your mind is always available. Take advantage of that today, and watch your leadership effectiveness skyrocket.

POWER POINT ELEVEN

ADMITTING MISTAKES

TURBO LEADERSHIP

52

I live by a simple way of thinking: When you mess up, 'fess up. Here's what I know about making mistakes: Be the first one to catch your mistake because others will catch it before you know it. Be the first person to bring your error to other people's attention. And, be the first one to say, "This is what happened, and this is what I'm going to do to correct it."

This does something powerful to your culture and your leadership. While your mistake is still a mistake, you gain equity in the middle of it. People see your honesty and feel empowered to fail forward—to 'fess up to their own mistakes without fear of retribution or judgment. You create an atmosphere that says, "When you make a mistake, it's just that—a mistake. Everybody makes them, and that's okay." Do your best not to make the same mistakes twice, of course. Try not to repeat your mistakes. But feel free to learn from them, and tell your team what you're going to do differently the next time.

I also encourage you to make new mistakes. The only people who don't are people who are not going anywhere, doing anything, saying anything, or being anybody. Do we really expect ourselves to learn new things, experience new highs, and take our organizations to new places without ever messing up? Or, if we're too afraid of mistakes, do we really expect ourselves not to move—never to go anywhere? Why would you want to live that kind of life? If you've been putting pressure on yourself or on others to live a mistake-free life, you need to know that there's no such thing. It doesn't exist.

That's why perfectionists never live perfect lives. The goal isn't to never mess up. It is to live a life of excellence. This allows you to keep growing, keep maturing, and keep going higher. You'll experience greater success and fulfillment in the midst of your mistakes. You'll have lessons to pass down, you'll have new memories and experiences to enjoy, and you'll be able to say that you persisted despite your slip-ups to achieve something truly significant.

That success will come at the cost of making mistakes. So make them! Don't repeat your previous mistakes; find new ones

MISTAKES TELL ME THAT YOU ARE DOING SOMETHING.

to make. Learn from others' errors, blunders, and missteps. 'Fess up when you mess up. Make solutions to your mistakes because mistakes tell me that you are doing something. Go easy on yourself when you mess up, and create a culture that will assure your team that you won't come after them when they mess up. The way to uncover the highest potential in your teammates is to allow them to fail and equip them to move forward with excellence when that happens. And to do that, you have to show them that you make mistakes, as well.

So what are you waiting for? Go make some new mistakes today.

So what are you waiting for? Go make some new mistakes today.

12

HELPING OTHERS

POWER POINT TWELVE

TURBO LEADERSHIP

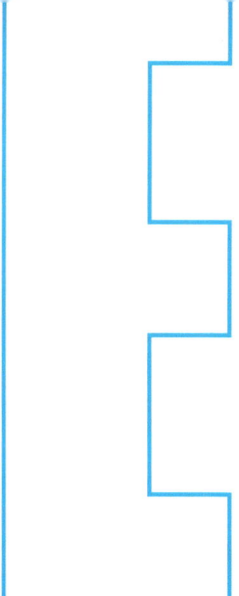

Every one of us is going to have many opportunities to help others. I don't care which country you are in or what your vocation is. You might work from home, take care of your family, or be surrounded by people all day long. No matter what you are a part of or where you live, one thing that all of us will have an opportunity to do today, and every day, is help others.

It could be as simple as letting somebody cut in front of you while sitting in traffic or as unpretentious as making sure that somebody has the resources they need to finish a project. You might be able to help somebody buy groceries. You might be able to offer a word of encouragement, a piece of advice, or a warning that saves someone trouble down the road. Help can come in different shapes and sizes, but helping others is your greatest opportunity.

So often, we assume that getting things done is paramount, but I'm going to suggest to you that helping others leads to more impactful leadership than simply checking things off of your list. When we focus on tasks above people, we lose touch with those on our teams and, ultimately, lose sight of the vision we set out to achieve. However, when we make others our priority, we'll see every area of our organization benefit: culture, leadership, our team's resourcefulness, and the overall morale. Someone helped you to get where you are today; your job as a leader is to equip, encourage, and empower those on your team in the same way.

When you offer assistance to others, you're not just helping them for today or making positive change in the present. There have been people in my life who helped me with a dollar bill here or a gallon of gas in my car there . . . who gave me some used tires or who bought me clothes. It doesn't have to be a grand or expensive gesture that you make. People helped me in the little things of life. And because of their support, today, I get to do what I'm doing all over the world. You never know how your actions will affect someone's legacy—where they will be years down the road. We hear stories all the time about how someone's mentor or role model showed them one act of kindness that had a ripple effect for generations to come.

> WHEN YOU OFFER ASSISTANCE TO OTHERS, YOU'RE NOT JUST HELPING THEM FOR TODAY.

Sometimes we overcomplicate helping others, and we underestimate the impact we'll have by making small decisions. Whether it's words or actions, help someone today, looking to the future and making sure you discern that what you're doing is ultimately for their good. Don't think short-term but long-term because your assistance can transform somebody's life. We all will have the opportunity to benefit somebody. Just do it.

13
GAINING CREDIBILITY

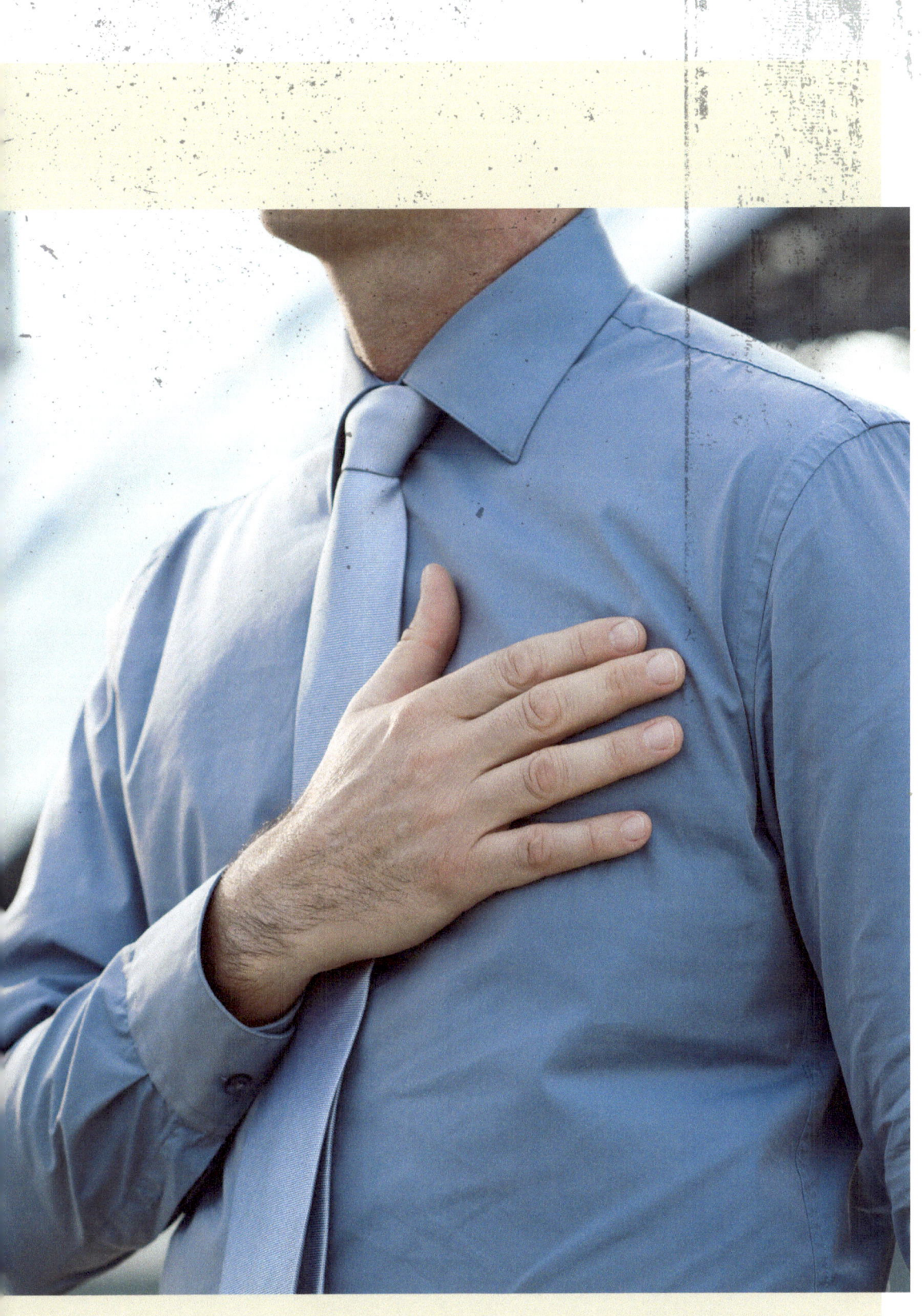

How do you gain credibility? How do you increase trust? How do you get people to believe in you? It's not by pretending to be something you're not. There is one simple answer to this question. It is the best way to gain credibility and build and keep trust. This simple answer is that you need to keep your promises.

I'm sure you've heard all about how to underpromise and over-deliver. People say that it's better to sell yourself short and then wow others with more than they expect than to talk yourself up and fall short of expectations. I'm in agreement with that principle, but what I mean by keeping your promises is that you simply do what you say you will do. You don't need to under- or over- anything. In fact, you need to be candid about what you're going to do—what's within your capacity and skill set to accomplish. This goes along with being honest with your team but extends beyond your organization to those you serve. If you make promises to your team and to your clients, make sure that those promises are within your ability to fulfill.

For example, if you make plans to meet someone at nine o'clock, be there at nine o'clock. If you say you are going to write that report, and it will be ready on Wednesday at ten o'clock, have the report ready on Wednesday at ten o'clock—or even before then. If you say you're going to send an email to somebody you met at a party, send that email. You said you were going to call somebody back? Call them back. Keep your promises. You said you were going to do something. Do it.

This builds the trust that people have in us, and it also builds our ability to gauge our own margin. If you're constantly overselling yourself, chances are that you don't truly know how much you're able to get done. If you're underselling yourself, you may not know where your limits are—when you need to stop, slow down, or take a break. But making and keeping promises empowers you to know where those lines are, how to communicate them effectively, and how to honor them. This sets you up to satisfy others

YOU SAID YOU WERE GOING TO DO SOMETHING. DO IT.

and yourself, making sure that everyone's happy, and you're able to be a healthy leader at the same time.

So often, people make promises and then break them without a second thought. The reality is that every unkept, broken promise adds to a person's lack of credibility, trust, and confidence from others. We've all been on the hurtful end of a broken promise. We know how much it stings. We know how we lose respect for or trust in the person. Most of the time, it's not about the big stuff. It's about the small stuff. You said you were going to be there. Are you going to be there?

Keep your promises, and you'll grow your credibility.

THE NEED FOR RESPECT

POWER POINT FOURTEEN

TURBO LEADERSHIP

66

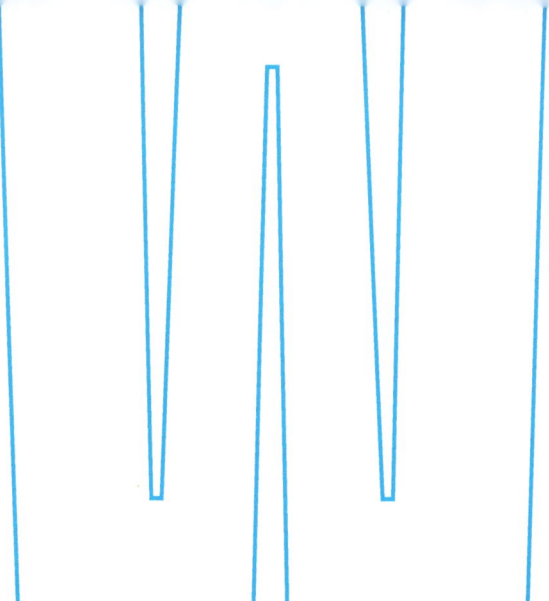

We were all born with an innate need for respect. Everybody wants to be respected. We crave it. Nobody likes being disrespected. Nobody likes being talked down to by others, dismissed by peers, friends, or coworkers—blown off. We all want to be valued, whether we are husbands and wives, employees and employers, or pastors and parishioners. Respect is wanted and needed on all sides of our organizations.

So, how do you get it? I'll give you a simple way to see more of it in your own life. Sow respect; reap respect. Give it; then, get respect. Respect is an echo. Think about it this way: Have you ever been in an empty room or at the bottom of the Grand Canyon? You've likely heard the sound of your voice or the click of your step reverberating back at you in such places. Respect works in a similar way. We often assume we can gain it without giving it, but the opposite is true. The more we disregard those around us—our families, our coworkers, our bosses, our peers—the less respect we garner for ourselves. Likewise, the more deference we show then, the more other people value and esteem us.

You've likely seen this in action. Think about the relationships in which you struggle to show respect. Chances are, the other person has not shown a wealth of regard for you. That doesn't

THE REAL QUESTION IS, AM I BEING RESPECTFUL?

necessarily mean their contempt for you is a direct result of yours for them, but the cycle feeds into itself until someone is brave enough to break it—to show honor even without receiving it.

The question, then, for each of us, is not, *Am I being respected?* The real question is, *Am I being respectful?* If I can show deference for somebody, I'm really saying something to them about myself. It reflects on my leadership and character—regardless of what they choose to do in return. We've given too much power to others over our responses and emotions. The truth is that we have a choice, no matter how we are treated, to treat others with dignity and class.

People who disregard others do so because, deep down, they harbor insecurities about themselves—or they're arrogant. People who devalue others are telling their own secrets! I'm willing to bet that many a time you've been disrespectful to someone else, it was due to a lack of confidence or identity inside of yourself. Maybe we don't realize this in the moment—we think it's all about them. They're the entire problem—but if we dig a bit deeper, we'll see that we each have our issues to work on.

Similarly, when you respect others, you're revealing to others a lot about yourself. You're telling them that you are secure, celebratory, and appreciative and that you realize it's not all about you. It's about everybody else. Sow respect; reap respect. Give respect; receive respect.

POWER POINT FIFTEEN

HANDLING CRITICISM

CONSTRUCTIVE CRITICISM IS ONLY CONSTRUCTIVE TO THE PERSON GIVING IT, BUT YOU AND I, ON THE RECEIVING END OF THINGS, HAVE A HARD TIME HANDLING THIS FEEDBACK.

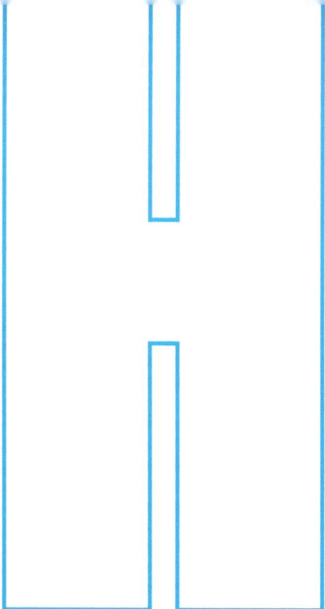

How do you handle criticism? This is something that everyone struggles with from time to time. No one is immune from receiving criticism, but it can be a challenge to handle it appropriately. I know you've had people walk up to you and say things like, "Hey, I want to give you some constructive criticism." Can I tell you a secret? There's no such thing as constructive criticism.

Constructive criticism is only constructive to the person giving it, but you and I, on the receiving end of things, have a hard time handling this feedback. We can smile. We can laugh about it. We can say, "Thank you so much. That was helpful." However, when you walk away from that person, your thoughts are often not the most charitable towards them.

So, what is the best way to handle other people's disapproval? How do we avoid getting an attitude towards the person displaying it? How do we give and receive criticism in a healthy, productive way? There is no simple answer to this question, but I can tell you what has been true in my life. Every time somebody has criticized me, I have had to pay attention to it. Even in my anger, disappointment, heartache, or bad attitude, I've had to think about what they said.

Many times, I could not reconcile their comments in that moment, but I came to understand them later. It has profited me in the long run, even though, in the moment, I didn't think it would do me any good. The truth is that the majority of people giving you truly helpful feedback are trying to benefit you. You may not understand why in the moment, but often, experience and time bring their wisdom to light. Maybe you can think back to a time you received a piece of criticism that only now makes sense since you're looking back from a place of more maturity. I bet you feel grateful that this person took the time to speak into your life, even if it wasn't pleasant.

I HAVE RECEIVED CRITICISM IN MY LIFE, AND MONTHS HAD TO GO BY— IN SOME CASES, YEARS—BEFORE IT MADE SENSE.

I have received criticism in my life, and months had to go by—in some cases, years—before it made sense. Then I'd think, *I see what she meant*. This has occurred many times. So, if I can just reflect on what has been happening, what was said to me, and receive it—by simply committing to think about it and do something with it—then I've come to a place in my life where I don't just discard criticism. I feel the present discomfort but know that down the road—for good or for worse—it will all make sense. Today's criticism can catapult your maturity. Do not brush it aside; store it for the future. And when you offer criticism to others, make sure that it will benefit them for years to come, as well.

16 SOLUTIONS

POWER POINT SIXTEEN

TURBO LEADERSHIP

74

There is one thing that can elevate you, get you noticed, cause you to be promoted, and even bring you more money through a raise. People pay exorbitant amounts of money to find out what it is, but I'm going to tell you for free. What is it? That one thing is a solution.

Every leader who's gotten higher in life was able to get there because of one thing—they brought solutions wherever they went. How did the head janitor become the head janitor? She or he started with a mop and a bucket, a vacuum cleaner, some spray, some towels, and some cleaning supplies, but then they started offering suggestions. They saw how to do things better, where money could be saved, how to do something faster or more efficiently, how to keep things clean before they got dirty, or how to manage supplies. They dealt in answers, and their superiors realized that they had more potential than they'd previously thought.

The same is true of every CEO, every pastor, and every head in an organization. We all start somewhere, but the key is what we do with the circumstances we're entrusted with by our leaders. You may be racking your brain trying to come up with remedies for whatever circumstance ails you; it may seem like the hand you've been dealt isn't ideal. That's a perfect opportunity for you to dig deeper and find the answers no one has thought of yet. If everything in your job ran smoothly, there would be little or no reason for your skill set and your unique gifts. You were placed there to find the solutions! You were placed where you are to offer up a new way of looking at things—a perspective no one can provide except you!

Wherever you are in life, in whatever capacity you are serving, your upward trajectory is all dependent on what you can offer. So when you're sitting in a meeting, and everybody's griping, moaning, growling, grumbling and complaining, you will be sitting there thinking, *I'm going to raise my hand and offer a solution.* You will be constantly thinking about fixes to the problems, needs, and challenges that arise in your organization. Why? Because you're a solution-oriented leader, and it's going to take you higher and farther faster.

EVERY LEADER WHO'S GOTTEN HIGHER IN LIFE WAS ABLE TO GET THERE BECAUSE OF ONE THING—THEY BROUGHT SOLUTIONS WHEREVER THEY WENT.

You've seen the opposite: individuals who do nothing but find what's wrong in a situation or an organization. While they may have influence over the tone of many conversations, their impact often isn't lasting. There's only so much you can talk about—then the need arises for some kind of plan, some kind of action. That is what you're in your position to provide!

Offer a solution. Others may not implement your idea. Your answer may not be the best, but at least you will not be lumped in with everybody else. And pretty soon, when you keep bringing solutions, ideas, and innovation, you'll get noticed. Everybody rises in life because of one thing: bringing solutions.

17

THE FIRST STEP

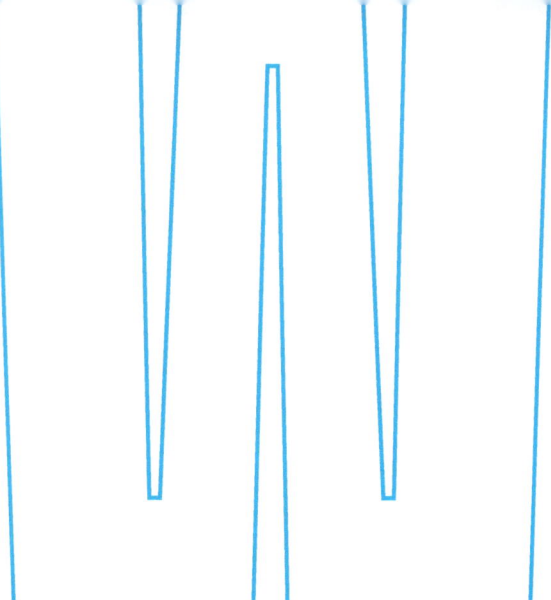

What is the first step towards growth? The first step towards learning? The first step towards maturity? The first step in your own personal journey that'll take you higher? Many people miss it, but it's not a complex idea.

It's a simple word called *humility*. All leaders that you see *have had to be* humble enough . . . *have to be* humble enough . . . and *must continue to be* humble enough to say, "I don't know that." "I need more information." "I need other people to help me with that." "I cannot do it by myself." "Oh, I need to learn some more about that." "I wonder how I didn't know about that." You get the idea. Think about some of your role models. Chances are they had to come to terms with the fact that they needed information, assistance, and input from those they respected. That's what leadership is, after all—bringing out the best in people and being willing to humbly learn from them.

There's not a human being on earth alive today who has learned all they will ever learn. Each day holds new opportunities, lessons, mistakes, and victories. To say you're finished learning—to adopt the opposite of a humble spirit—is to say that you're done truly living! So how do we begin to change the culture of leadership, starting with ourselves?

Humility starts off in a deficit position. Humility starts with you saying to yourself and me saying to myself, *I don't know. I need others. I need to know more.* Proud people will never confess that. Arrogant people will never embrace that. However, the first step towards maturity, growth, learning, and increase is acknowledging that you don't know. We call that being consciously incompetent: *I know that I don't know.* If you inwardly balk at that revelation, ask yourself why. Who are the voices in your past who made you feel ashamed for not knowing something? Maybe it's your own inner voice. Maybe you had a parent or friend who ridiculed you for not knowing it all, not being prepared, or not being able to do it yourself. It's imperative that we do the work to uncover our scars so that we can move forward in confidence *and* humility. When we accept that we don't know everything, we can drop the immense weight of having to have it all together, and we can truly learn from those around us.

> **THE FIRST STEP TOWARDS MATURITY, GROWTH, LEARNING, AND INCREASE IS ACKNOWLEDGING THAT YOU DON'T KNOW.**

When I know that I don't know, it causes a spirit and an attitude of humility that's willing to benefit from whomever can help me. I start to see others in a new light and myself in a new light, as well. Your best steps, your highest steps, and your growth in your personal and professional lives will start the day when you are humble enough to say, "I need to know more."

18
ELOQUENT LISTENING

POWER POINT EIGHTEEN

There is a skill I like to practice called eloquent listening. You may be thinking that the word *eloquent* is about speaking, and the word *listening* is on the other side of the spectrum. You may consider this phrase and conclude that it doesn't make sense—that they don't go together. Eloquent listening is just my personal term for what some people call active listening. It is so important, when you are listening to somebody, to not insert yourself into their story. This takes an emotional and mental maturity that many of us have not developed, but it's so rewarding that it's worth taking the time and energy to cultivate. What's the alternative? Listening simply in order to respond.

You've had friends do this. I've had friends do this. You're sharing a vulnerable or interesting part of yourself, and their immediate response—sometimes what they even interrupt you with—is a similar account from their own lives. "Oh! I had a work situation like that." "Well, *my* kids are even more difficult." "Oh, just wait until you get promoted." While their intentions may be neutral or even benevolent, they too often hasten to reply without truly considering the needs and the words of the person doing the speaking. We're just as guilty of this in our own experiences, as much as we may hate to admit it.

Have you ever noticed that when somebody's telling a story about themselves—their mother, their kids, how they used to live in a different state, used to drive a certain car, or have a specific job—your own story starts percolating in your mind? You think of a time you felt the same way, had the same struggle, won the same fight, or encountered a piece of wisdom that helped you and could *really* help this person in their scenario. If you're not careful, you'll end up telling them your story and brushing right past what they're thinking and feeling. Instead of truly listening, you jump to responding.

IT IS SO IMPORTANT, WHEN YOU ARE LISTENING TO SOMEBODY, TO NOT INSERT YOURSELF INTO THEIR STORY.

It happens to me too. I find myself doing that all the time. It's human nature, on some level. However, as soon as you insert yourself into their story, you are losing what they are trying to tell you. You miss their unique perspective. Their unique gifts. Their unique experience. Their unique wisdom. There could be something you're meant to glean from that conversation that you'll completely miss—and what's more, you'll be missing the truest, deepest connection with that person because you're not fully tuned in and listening to what they have to say.

It happens every day. People are going to tell you different things. It doesn't matter who you are—somebody's going to tell you about an experience. They went shopping here; they went eating there. They traveled there, or they bought this thing. Whatever they tell you, don't insert yourself into their story. Be an eloquent listener.

GENERATING NEW THOUGHTS

POWER POINT NINETEEN

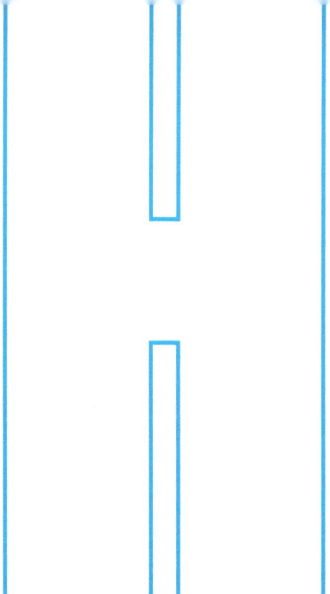

How do you generate new thoughts? How do you think yourself out of a conundrum, come up with novel ideas, and brainstorm solutions to complex problems?

In my life experience, new thoughts have not come from within me. New thoughts have to be catalyzed, instigated—even provoked—by sources outside of me. This means they come from what I'm reading, listening to, watching on TV, or pulling up on my phone or computer on any given day. New thoughts come from my conversations with people, whether they be coaching clients, CEOs, friends, or neighbors. As I observe the world around me, everything can be an instructive tool.

We often look past minutiae throughout our day, focused on our goals and objectives. But did you know that many of those overlooked details may offer you a key insight that could solve the problems you're so preoccupied with? There are always different vantage points from which to see things and new experiences and walks of life that we can observe and empathize with. People around us have so much richness to offer us if we'll take the time to study our surroundings and interact with them.

The challenge with new thoughts is that we have a filter in our heads, and this filter has a way of getting rid of new thoughts. We cling habitually to the familiar. Your mind's filter will tell you why this new thought is not the right one, why it's not the right time, why you don't have this, or why you don't qualify for that. And just as you are receiving new thoughts, there are these disqualifiers popping into your head. It's an almost instantaneous process and one we'll miss if we're not attuned to our thought patterns.

Deaden the sound. Dull the noise in your head. Take that previously undiscovered idea seriously. Study it. Wonder about it. Be curious about it. Ask others about it. Read books on the topic. Listen to podcasts. Take a walk outside, and mull it over in your mind. Think, strategize, pray, and get counsel about it. Fresh consideration of that concept may make it happen for you. It may lead to a breakthrough in your job, character growth in an area of your heart, or a brand-new relationship with an expert you'd never met before.

THERE ARE ALWAYS DIFFERENT VANTAGE POINTS FROM WHICH TO SEE THINGS AND NEW EXPERIENCES AND WALKS OF LIFE THAT WE CAN OBSERVE AND EMPATHIZE WITH.

You are going to come across information and perspectives you've never considered before. Cultivate them because notions don't just come into our lives for their own sake. They are for the purpose of helping you go higher, so you help others to go higher, as well. What are you thinking about today? Write it down, spend time with it, and use it to enhance your leadership.

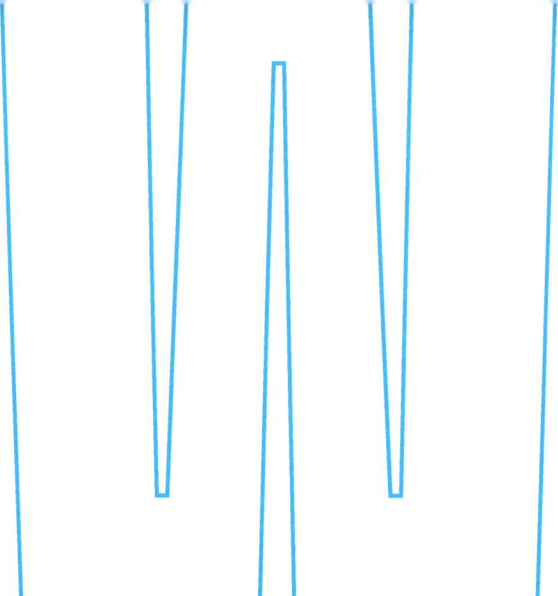

We want others to do it, but we don't want to do it ourselves.

What is it?

Change.

We want others to change—their minds, their viewpoints, their actions, their habits, their way of speaking—but we think we personally are okay. Here are a few aspects of change that I think are important to know. They've helped me on my own journey, and I know they'll help you as you consider the importance of doing, being, and seeing differently.

All transformation is about loss. Therefore, whenever you ask someone to change, you're asking them to give up something. They have to let go of the old way in order to take hold of the new way. This doesn't come easily to any of us, so be sure to have grace when you bring a need for change to someone's attention. Allow time for them to see, consider, and adjust accordingly.

Also, any suggestion for change is a critique of the past. If I move a table from one side of the room to the other because I don't like where it used to be, I've evaluated its position and determined that another is better. All change is like that. Some people may take this more personally than you intend it to be. When you propose something different, be sure to do it in a way that affirms the person, honors their past, and encourages them to step into

YOU HAVE TO UNDERSTAND THE VALUE OF TAKING PEOPLE ON **THE JOURNEY.**

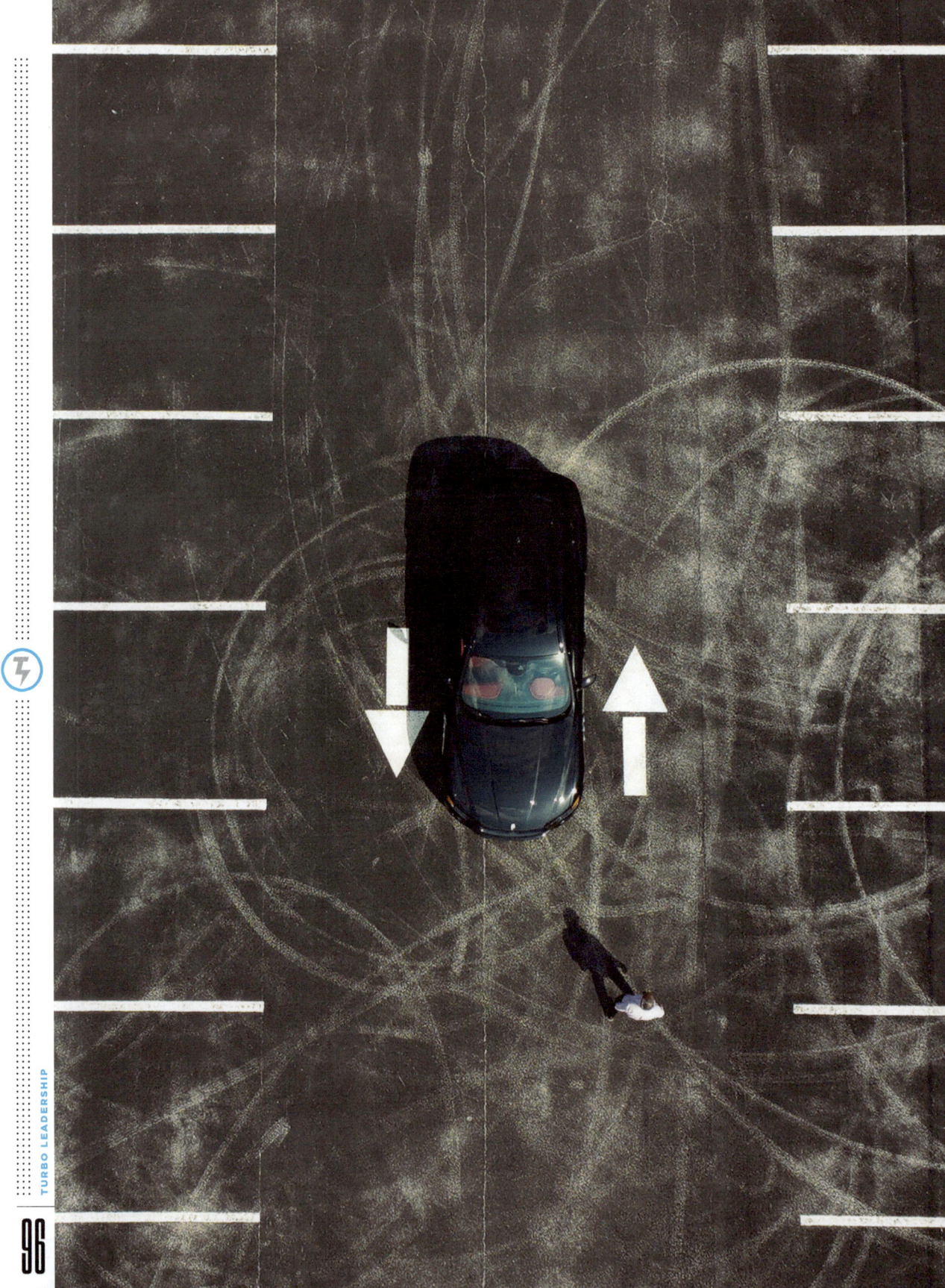

new ways of doing things for their own good. Depending on your tone, you can either communicate that you're against their past or that you desire to build upon it for a brighter future.

Further, when you impose change, remind yourself of this universal truth, no matter your leadership role: Change *imposed* is change *opposed*. What is it about anything different that people resist? What is it that *I* resist? We all are change-resistant. We cling to our scruples at almost any cost, overly critical of new ways of going about life. Why? It is because we were not taken on the journey of arrival. This is something a leader can do quite manageably, but too few leaders make the effort. Most people come in and announce a change without any other preparation, but if you

YOU ARRIVED AT THAT POINT OF CHANGE YOU'RE PROMOTING VIA A JOURNEY OF YOUR OWN.

are leading an organization—if you are leading anything at all—you have to understand the value of taking people on the journey.

You arrived at that point of change you're promoting via a journey of your own. Before you make an announcement about any adjustment, modification, or transition, give your people time to process it. If you can allow them to trod the path to your destination, you'll find not only that resistance decreases but that the ownership of change will come about more easily in your organization. The bottom line is that leaders must consider the dynamics of any change and act accordingly.

21

POWER POINT TWENTY-ONE

LEARNING FROM DISAPPOINTMENTS

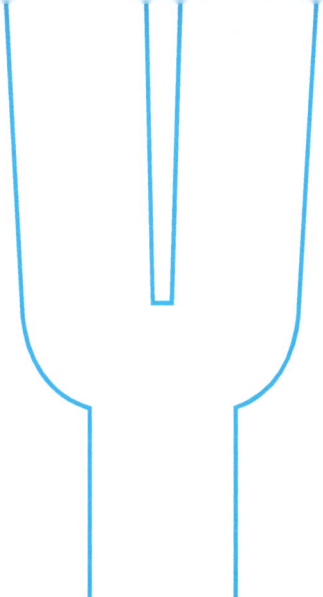

You've heard phrases like these tossed around: "Be a lifelong learner."

"Be a perpetual learner."

"I'm always learning."

It's easy to make these claims but not truly be learning. That's why, today, I want to share the *value* of learning with you. When you make it a priority to continuously put yourself in a position of discovery, it becomes a sort of muscle in you. You strengthen it over time, exercising it in situations where you encounter new information, adversity, or a change in course.

It's only when you look at wherever you are, accept it, and begin trying to glean knowledge from everything that you will begin to understand the *value* of learning. Everything becomes instructive, a lesson, something that you can gain from in the long run. You begin to see resources and potential you didn't before that you can "plug and play" at another time.

Have you ever been in a situation in which a disappointment taught you a valuable lesson? Some of our most character-forming moments occur when we have to change course, reevaluate, and admit that we failed. This, too, is fertile soil for learning new

lessons—in maturity, endurance, and resilience. We learn what to avoid in the future.

At first, we don't enjoy learning this way, but in the long run, it's the best thing for us. If we never suffer disappointment, we'll never truly grow in those areas. We'll always assume we've got it all together, and we won't ask for help, be humbled, or rethink our strategy for the better.

So the value of learning shows itself when you stop long enough to say to yourself, *What have I learned today? Where have I grown?* When you become a perpetual learner, you don't see circumstances as adverse. You understand that you're in a position that has led you to consider the world differently. You do not see a situation outside of your control. You see one that will provide you with a different perspective. When you have a setback, you view it as an opportunity to become wiser—sharper—because that is the only way a person can handle these lessons. Change your mindset in this area, and you'll accelerate your development tenfold. You'll bounce back from disappointments much more quickly and turn them around into lessons and victories in an effective manner. What's more, you'll be able to help those you lead see frustrations as opportunities, too. And that's one of the hallmarks of a truly effective leader.

Things *will* happen in your life. You will like some of them, and you won't like others. My question for you at the end of the day will be, "Did you learn anything? If you did, what was it?" There's value in constant learning.

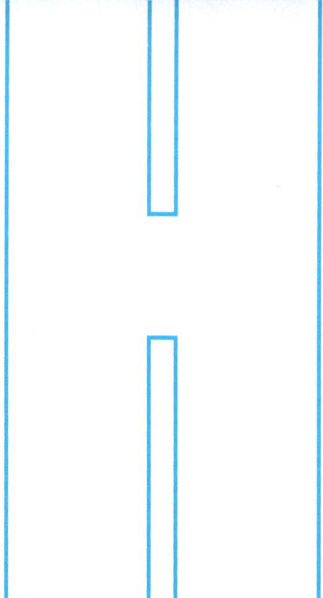

How do you deal with underperforming people? To answer this question, we need to start with a definition of underperforming people. These are people who do not meet expectations. You may give them a task, but it doesn't get done. You give them a deadline, but it doesn't get met. These people always have reasons and excuses. They don't seem to care about what you say, and they're not making an effort to improve themselves. They don't come through. Underperforming people make promises but can't keep them. You had high expectations, but you're not getting what you think you should from them. Does that sound like someone you deal with? Maybe you've seen a trend on your team that sounds familiar to this.

Before you get a bad attitude—which you probably already have—and before you fire this person—because I know you are already thinking about that—or before you do even worse…move them from one department to the other—because that is spreading toxicity—I have a suggestion for you. Create an improvement plan.

An improvement plan comes into being when you or someone you delegate that job to sits down with the underperformer and begins to formulate a plan. This takes intentionality and energy which are what our human nature doesn't want to invest in these underperformers. However, it's the only way to figure out if they're truly capable and if we've given them all that we can. What does an improvement plan look like, exactly? How do you structure it when there are already expectations that aren't being met?

Present the five areas in which you want to see improvement from this person. Then, give him or her six months to show development in each one of them. Create a system by which these improvements can be put down in writing, so you have a record of them. It's important to include the specific benchmarks you're looking for—how you will measure that improvement—in order to put metrics behind it. Without these, it will be difficult for the person to know how to improve on a day-to-day basis. Have somebody meet with this person every month to see if they are improving—if the needle is moving on the dashboard of their improvement plan. By the time you get to months four and five, you will know whether they're a keeper or if you need to release them.

HAVE CLEAR, WRITTEN BENCHMARKS AND METRICS (IN YOUR IMPROVEMENT PLAN).

By the time you get to the sixth month, the jury will come back with a simple verdict. Don't wait until the six-month mark. Measure their progress consistently. Have this conversation with them every month. Have clear, written benchmarks and metrics as well as somebody to guide the process. Before you shuttle the underperformer out of your organization, give them the tools and the resources to improve themselves. If they do so, good. If they don't, you know what to do next.

23
SUSTAINING MOMENTUM

POWER POINT TWENTY-THREE

TURBO LEADERSHIP

108

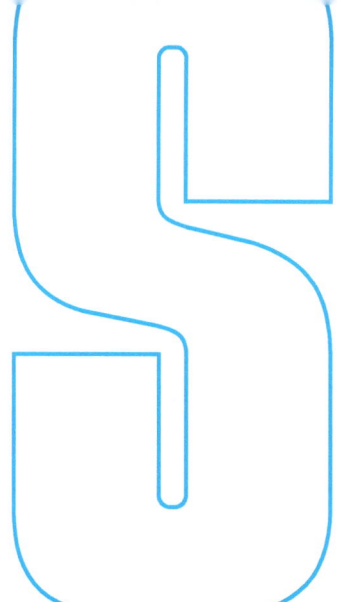

Sustaining momentum is difficult to do. It is not initiating, obtaining, or gaining momentum but sustaining it that proves challenging. Why is this? Let me explain.

Momentum is a great exaggerator. It is going to make you look better than you really are—more effective, more efficient. However, the flip side of that coin is that it can make things look *worse* than they really are, too. People will say things such as, "Our company is—or our church is—gaining momentum." "Our company's—or our church's—momentum is declining." Everything gains or loses momentum, and that shifts the way we view the seasons in our organizations.

A few examples of specific things that spur growth are messaging, conversations, and alliances—these all affect the level of active engagement for you and your team. On the positive side of things, the question that will help you to build good motion is this: "How do we maintain this forward growth?" You may laugh at the answer I'm going to share with you because it seems easier and simpler than one would assume; however, as it's coming from somebody who does this for a living, I trust that you'll at least consider it. Here it is: You sustain momentum by doing the basics. Just do the basics.

Remember when your church was smaller? Do you recall when you were an emerging leader? Remember when you were just launching a company, and you could only do the basics, such as calling people back in a timely manner or not letting details slip by. Basics, for you at the start, meant not delaying action when you needed to take it, making key decisions instead of kicking the ball down the field, and being proactive in showing people how much you value them. These are just the essentials. It sounds oversimplified, but many of us lose sight of what really matters as we start to take on speed. The irony in this is that those actions are what contributed to your gaining ground in the first place, and you cannot maintain any kind of positive, forward motion without sustaining them.

YOU SUSTAIN MOMENTUM BY DOING THE BASICS.

I am confounded at times when I look at churches, corporations and organizations—for-profit as well as nonprofit—who think they are beyond the basics. You will *never* get beyond the basics. We have amazing airplanes flying in the air, but the essentials are still the same—lift, gravity, and aerodynamics have not changed. We have beautiful tapestries and paintings, but the artistic elements are still the same: color, texture, and depth. We have symphonies composed for piano and all kinds of orchestral instruments, but the fundamentals are the same: octaves, notes, and the like. The basics do not change. So if you really want to sustain momentum, don't ever forget the values, ideals, and rudimentary disciplines that you started with—they're the key to moving forward.

THE BASICS DO NOT CHANGE.

SO IF YOU REALLY WANT TO SUSTAIN MOMENTUM, DON'T EVER FORGET THE VALUES, IDEALS, AND RUDIMENTARY DISCIPLINES THAT YOU STARTED WITH— THEY'RE THE KEY TO MOVING FORWARD.

POWER POINT TWENTY-FOUR

24 WHAT IS AND WHAT IF

TURBO LEADERSHIP | 114

There are two questions that I've heard asked by two types of people. Both of these questions are important, but depending on which one you ask, it can either keep you where you are or take you somewhere new. One kind of person asks the question, "What is . . . ?" The other asks, "What if . . . ?"

"What is?" and "What if?"

"What is" questions deal with present realities—they speak of things in the here and now—today. They deal with data. These inquiries tell you where you are at this moment, but they don't provide you with any leverage for movement. "What is" questions merely give you information. This could encompass the numbers in your organization: payroll, profit, sales, expenditures, etc. It could include the personal interests and spending patterns you've discovered about your customers and clients or comprise reviews and feedback as to your operations. It could be the metrics by which you measure success and how you've been doing on achieving your goals up to the present.

Movement, on the other hand, comes from people who ask the second question: "What if . . . ?" This way of thinking draws from one's imagination. It is generated in your brain as well as from your information and your data. "What if" questions indicate curiosity about what you could do and revolve around future moves: locations, team members, clientele, new ventures—anything that's not currently in existence but that could become a reality if you decided to act on it.

In truth, you need both "what is" and "what if" in order to move forward with wisdom and bravery. Data without imagination is doomed to stagnation, and imagination without facts won't yield results that endure or stay effective in the long run. "What is" can be a starting point; however, beware of leaning only on particulars. If you are going to keep your vision under the control of what is, then your reality will always define your future. And here's a secret I've learned: your reality is *never* your future because your future is greater than your present reality.

YOUR REALITY IS NEVER YOUR FUTURE BECAUSE YOUR FUTURE IS GREATER THAN YOUR PRESENT REALITY.

Your present finances, team, location—everything in your present—is dynamic. It's not static. It's going to be moving, but it'll move only if you have people, including yourself, who will ask, "What if?" This is the power of imagination. "What if we could do this?" "What if we stopped this?" "What if we started that?" "What if we let this person go?" "What if we hired that person?" "What if we move this person from here to there?"

"What is" will keep you where you are. "What if" will take you where you're going. When you create a culture that asks the right question, your future will not be confined to a small box. Your future's limits are as high as the sky because you ask the right question which is, "What if . . . ?"

IF YOU ARE GOING TO KEEP YOUR VISION UNDER THE CONTROL OF

25
THINKING NEW

POWER POINT TWENTY-FIVE

TURBO LEADERSHIP

120

THINKING NEW

I know this about myself: I'm a creature of habit. I form patterns. I have routines. I have my schedule, and I like to stick to it when I can. I have my favorite places to go, things to eat, and people to spend time with. I have my favorite work rhythms and methods of getting things done.

This isn't just me that I'm talking about, however. This describes you, as well. The questions for all of us to ask ourselves are, *What will keep me from going where I want to go? What will keep me from achieving what I want to achieve? What will keep me from accomplishing what I feel is within my grasp to accomplish?* The answer is simple: It will be my lack of new thinking.

I have found this, and perhaps you have found this to be true, too: new thinking does not arise from inside of me. I don't naturally gravitate to new ideas, methods, and strategies. Rather, new thinking has always come from people outside of me. I've encountered it in coaching sessions, seminars, one-on-one conversations, books, podcasts, and many other places. New people have brought me ideas on a variety of topics. New people have brought me opportunities in a multitude of areas. New thinking comes with new people, and new people ask you questions that others have not asked you yet. New people give you options you were not thinking of before they stepped into your life. New people make you think new thoughts.

Who in your world is making you think new?

Your new thinking is going to take you to your future. There is nothing wrong with your old thinking . . . if you want to stay exactly where you are today. But to go forward, you have to have new thinking, and your new thinking will come from new thinkers. Who are the new thinkers in your life? Maybe it's a coworker you haven't gotten to know very well, the barista at your favorite coffeehouse, a family member you've lost touch with over the years, or a friend you meet at the gym or on the golf course. No matter who those new people are, embrace new relationships, and welcome the new thinking that they provide for you every day. Be looking

NEW PEOPLE ASK YOU QUESTIONS THAT OTHERS HAVE NOT ASKED YOU YET.

out for the conversations that will yield those new thoughts, and do your part to foster them.

I have found this: You don't have to agree with another person in order to learn from them. Isn't that a novel concept? What if we all realized this truth? People with different worldviews, opinions, and viewpoints make us think in ways we would not have otherwise—and that's a good thing! Some of the most abrasive people in my life have taught me more about myself than the nice people have taught me. Some of the most beneficial relationships you have will challenge, mold, and sharpen you. For your future to be new, you need new thinking.

I have been around leadership experts, in leadership conversations, and at leadership events for most of my life. I've seen much of the behind-the-scenes of the art of leadership, and I've noticed something over the years.

Great intentions abound. People aim to do this, or they mean to do that. The intent is there—and I think most people have good intentions, but intentions alone accomplish nothing. You've probably had a plan to do something positive in your own life. Maybe you want to get back to the gym and get in better shape, increase the amount of time you spend on your hobbies, launch a new business, unveil a new product, or form a new partnership. Maybe you want to eat more healthily or spend more time with your family. We've all seen the results of good intentions that have no action behind them. These noble objectives simply don't materialize in our lives.

Impact is what it means to put those intentions into practice. It is taking the idea that you have and forming a plan to ensure that it becomes a reality. Impact is taking what you are thinking and saying, *What is it that I really want to achieve?* You need both, but you have to start with impact in order to truly see the results you want. Why is that?

Most people do not move from intent to impact because they did not start with impact. Here are a few questions for you: What is it you really want to achieve or you are really trying to accomplish? What is your end goal, and what will that do for you in your organization, your life, or your relationships? It matters. When you start with impact and not just intent, your path will be clear to you. Intent is merely acquiescing to going in a certain direction, but it doesn't achieve anything.

If I were to come to your organization as a consultant, I would see that you have established a set of good intentions. However, the reason you would have brought me in is because you wouldn't be having the impact you desired to have. So the question is not, "What is our intent?" The questions should be, "What is our

IMPACT IS (PUTTING YOUR INTENTIONS) INTO PRACTICE.

impact?" "How will we know when we're truly achieving it?" "How will we measure it?" "What will the outcome be if our impact is fully accomplished?" "How will that impact take us to the next impact we want to make?"

Intentions are okay. They'll make you feel good and give you a false sense of momentum. However, impact is what's going to truly change your life. Combine these two, and you'll be able to go anywhere you want, achieve any goal, meet any quota, or solidify any team.

What are your intentions, and how do you plan to achieve them and impact your world?

WHEN YOUR VISION IS GREATER THAN YOUR RESOURCES

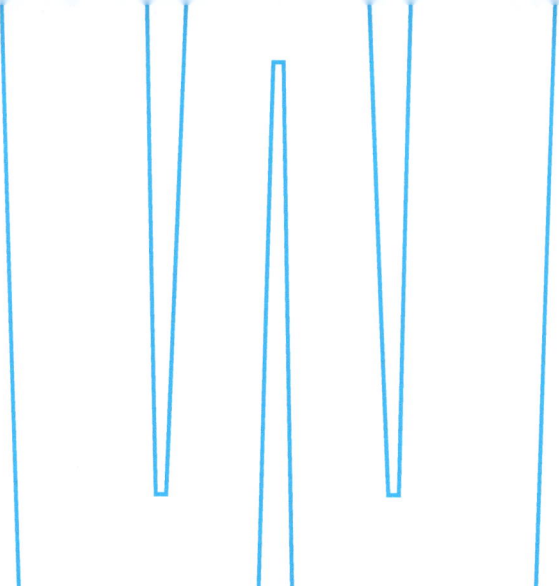

When your vision is greater than your resources, what do you do?

First of all, my belief on the matter is that it should always be this way. If your resources are larger than your vision, your vision is not good enough. It's not big enough, expansive enough, or ambitious enough. It is not reaching where it needs to reach. Any growing organization has the same dilemma. Their vision is always going to be greater than their resources. Otherwise, we stagnate. We all know companies or individuals without vision—they're directionless. They don't know where they need to be, so they don't know what they need to do. On the opposite end of the spectrum, many of our friends and colleagues are full of vision but don't have the resources to make it a reality right now. Here's a trick to fixing this problem.

First of all, what are your resources? Let me remind you that your greatest resources are not your facilities . . . or your money . . . or your organization . . . or your products, services, and processes. Your greatest resource is your *people* because none of those other resources can accomplish anything if there is not a person putting them to use.

Further, the greatest resource you need for the fulfillment of your vision is going to be the right people in the right places. Too often, we don't have the right people, or we have the right people, but we haven't strategically placed them where they will have the most impact. How do we correct these oversights?

These are the questions you need to ask yourself: *Who are the right people for my organization? What gifts do they have? What resources do they bring? How can I leverage their gifts, resources, talents, passions, commitments, and loyalties to further my vision? What position most brings out their abilities and makes the most of them for my organization?*

This won't just benefit you as the leader—it will ensure a happier, more fulfilled staff or team, as well. We've all known people

YOUR GREATEST RESOURCE IS YOUR PEOPLE.

who worked a job where their passions, gifts, and talents were not being maximized. We've probably even felt that way in a job ourselves at some point in time. When each team member knows they are essential and that the roles you've placed them in have been thought through—that they are making the biggest difference right where they are and that the difference they're making will have lasting repercussions—they'll truly give it their all.

Your people will take you higher. Or, if you aren't strategically placing them, your people will stagnate and bring you low. It's all about the people. So, when your resources do not match your vision, focus not on things but on people.

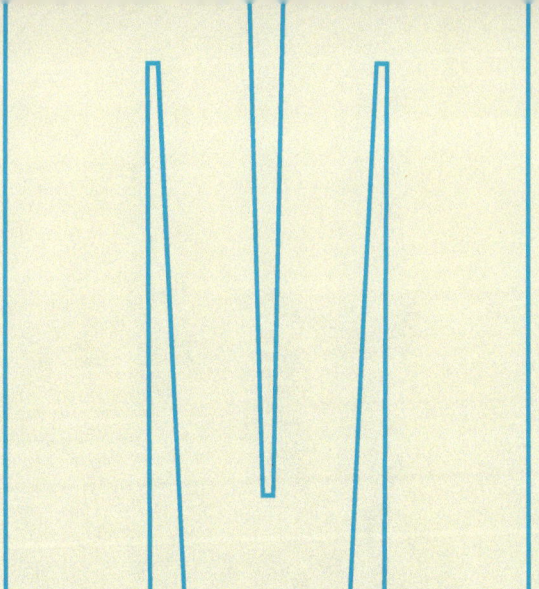

Most leaders don't think about their style of leadership because they evolve from one style to another style to another style. These leaders never consciously stop and ask themselves, *How has my leadership style changed?* While, on the surface, we might assume that it's best to have no changes in our leadership styles, I would argue that your leadership style cannot be static. It has to be dynamic. We simply have to be aware of how we and the world around us are changing and adjust our methods of leading accordingly.

I started my leadership journey many years ago, in the early seventies. I had a style then, but my age and season of life have caused my leadership style to evolve in the years since. I've heard new voices, listened to new leaders, read new methodologies, studied new theories, and experienced the highs and lows of leading teams. I've learned so much since I began that it wouldn't make sense for me to have the same mindset about leadership today that I had fifty years ago.

My principles are still the same, but my thought patterns, processes, and views of life and my environment have shifted. The way I view options, alternatives, and possibilities has changed.

YOUR STYLE OF LEADERSHIP

YOUR LEADERSHIP STYLE

So, my style of leadership has to change as well. It's not about the substance of your leadership but the style of your leadership. Let me put it this way: If your style is not congruent with your status in life right now, then you will not be able to move forward. You'll be stuck in the past or stuck reaching forward to a place you haven't arrived yet, confused about why you aren't able to make any progress. We have to be honest with ourselves about who we are and where we are if we want to be effective.

A leader whose style is divorced from his or her stage of life comes across as shallow or superficial. Most people can tell when he or she is putting on a façade, trying to be someone they're not. What's more, the people you serve and lead need an ever-maturing, ever-evolving leader; therefore, when we refuse to move forward

CANNOT BE STATIC. IT HAS TO BE DYNAMIC.

in our style, not only are we doing ourselves a disservice—we're not serving our people to the full extent that we could be.

If you had a smaller company and now you have a larger company—or if you had a smaller church and now you have a larger church—you have made changes to your leadership style. It goes without saying. The proof is in the pudding. That reality simply means that your style of leadership has adapted and adjusted to where you are.

Ask yourself this simple question: *How has my style changed over the last ten years?* And once you become conscious of your leadership style, you'll be able to keep evolving into the next style of leadership awaiting you.

POWER POINT TWENTY-NINE

29
INTERNAL CONFLICT

TURBO LEADERSHIP

138

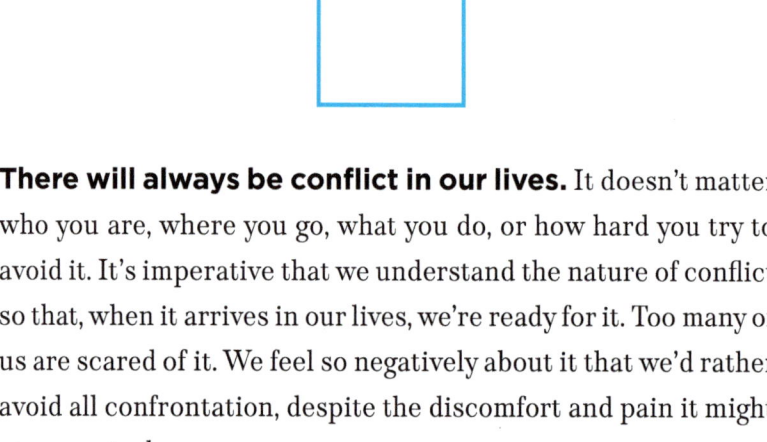

There will always be conflict in our lives. It doesn't matter who you are, where you go, what you do, or how hard you try to avoid it. It's imperative that we understand the nature of conflict so that, when it arrives in our lives, we're ready for it. Too many of us are scared of it. We feel so negatively about it that we'd rather avoid all confrontation, despite the discomfort and pain it might cause us to do so.

Here's a truth I've picked up in my own leadership journey: Conflict is neutral, normal, and natural. Neutral, normal, and natural. Doesn't that make it seem a bit less threatening?

While conflict is everywhere, there are two different kinds of conflict in every organization. One is internal conflict; the other is external conflict. They have different appearances and results, and here's what I've seen. Most of the leaders I've worked with in my coaching and encountered in my life perceive and move towards external conflict. They approach it, confront it, lean into it, and fix it. They take care of external conflict. After all, the personal cost is fairly cheap. At most, we might lose some face or have to admit that we were wrong about a certain fact or discussion point.

The conundrum for me is that I'm around leaders on a regular basis who know that internal conflict is simmering among their staff, festering on their board, and boiling just below the surface with their trustees, deacons, volunteers, or whatever teams make up their organizations. They see it, but they don't do anything about it. They talk to me when I come in to coach them, and they tell me about the people who don't get along or the people who are passive-aggressive towards others. They see what one person is doing to another person or how someone is sabotaging the group as a whole. They see all that, but they don't do anything about it. Why do they refrain from making the difference their position empowers them to make in these situations? Simply put: Because it is messy. We don't like mess. We don't want to get our hands

INTERNAL CONFLICT IS CARBON MONOXIDE.

dirty, and we don't like to dive into the office politics and power struggles that are the occupational hazards of working with other human beings.

This is what you need to know, though: Internal conflict is carbon monoxide. It's deadly. You neither smell it nor see it, but it is a killer nonetheless, and it is going to kill you more quickly and mercilessly than its external counterpart. So it's up to you to do the hard work. Deal with it, and figure it out. Don't live with it any longer because it's the death by a thousand cuts that will take you down in the long run.

30
SAFE ZONE TO BRAVE ZONE

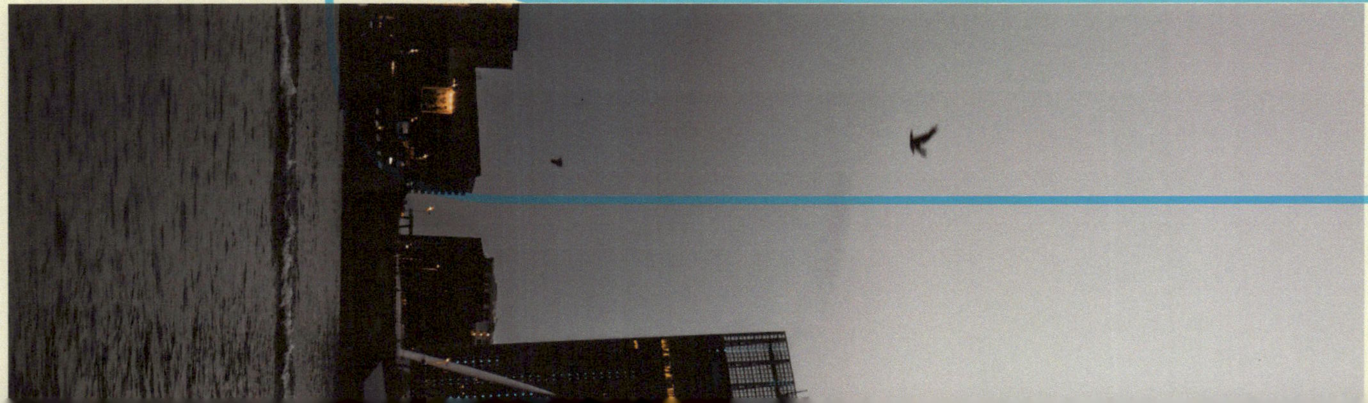

POWER POINT THIRTY

TURBO LEADERSHIP

144

SAFE ZONE TO BRAVE ZONE

145

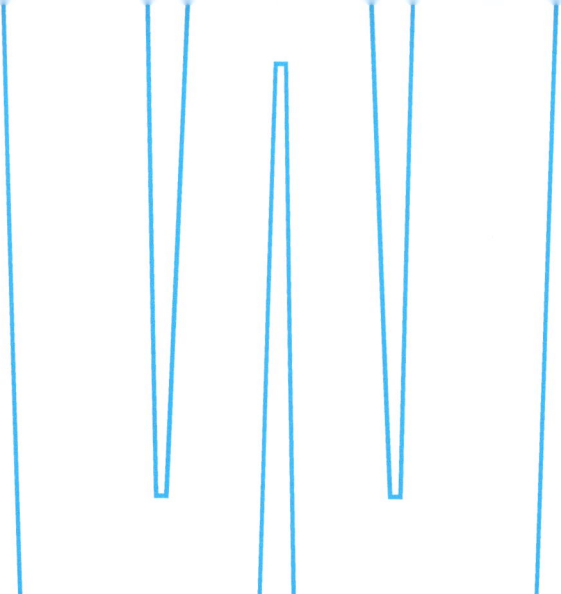

What does it mean to move from the safe zone to the brave zone? In the safe zone, you know the outcomes; they're a known quantity. The safe zone involves very little risk because you've been there before. You know what you're getting into because routine rules in the safe zone. You have friends who have been with you, tell you exactly what to do when a problem arises, and bail you out if you need it. That's the safe zone. Many of us spend years here because it comes naturally, and we don't know many people who are willing to venture outside of it.

On the flip side, there's the brave zone. The brave zone is where you haven't been before—it's new territory. You end up there when you make a point to go beyond your current resources or invite new voices to speak into your life—voices who might have things to say that could hurt in the short term. The brave zone is engaging in ways of thinking that might be new to you—even ways that go against your current convictions. It's where the most effective leaders live—I'd argue that it's where all true leaders live. After all, anybody can live in the safe zone.

As a leader, you have to live in the brave zone because leadership is not maintaining. It's not upholding the status quo,

YOU DIDN'T GET WHERE YOU ARE TODAY BY LIVING IN THE SAFE ZONE.

encouraging people to avoid doing any real work, keeping things the way they are today, and hoping that some mysterious force will take you somewhere higher, better, or more effective. Leadership is leading. It is challenging the status quo, pushing yourself and those you lead outside of your collective and individual comfort zones, and having the courage to press the boundaries of what you've known to be possible for your organization. In the brave zone, you need that ingredient known as courage. Only courageous, tenacious leadership makes any difference in one's sphere of influence.

So, while everything within you and your organization wants to retreat to the safe zone, keep reminding yourself that you didn't get where you are today by living in the safe zone. You achieved the victories, made the strides, and learned the lessons because

MOVE DEEPER WITH GREATER DARING AND COURAGE BECAUSE YOU HAVE GOTTEN TO WHERE YOU ARE BY STEPPING OUT AGAIN AND AGAIN.

you stepped outside of your comfort zone—directly into the brave zone. Don't make your brave zone your safe zone—don't be satisfied with how far you've come. Keep flourishing, increasing, and resourcing. Pour more into your people and yourself. Move deeper with greater daring and courage because you have gotten to where you are by stepping out again and again—out of the safe zone and into the brave zone.

Do you feel stuck?

All of us have been there before, at one time or another. It could be a setback in your personal life, a roadblock your organization has come up against, something on your team that's holding you back, or any number of obstacles leading you to feel this way. The feeling in itself isn't the enemy, and it's not inherently bad. In fact, it can actually help catapult you forward.

I want to suggest that when you feel stuck, you cannot get unstuck from the inside. You can only get unstuck from the outside. Let me explain what I mean by this.

At one time, I lived in Michigan. There were a few times when my car went into the ditch on icy, snowy, slippery roads. I had wheels on my car. I had gas in my car. I had a steering wheel. I had an accelerator . . . all of the essentials, right? But once I was in the ditch, I was stuck. I could not simply drive myself out of the ditch. Do you know what I had to do? I had to call a tow truck.

A tow truck came, hooked itself up to my car, and pulled me out of the ditch. It got me unstuck. If you're feeling stuck right now, your help will come from somebody on the outside. I don't know what that means in your context—you have a greater grasp on what it looks like since you're the one in your own shoes. But somebody from the outside will be able to help you. They can come, hook up their chain, and pull you out of your ditch. The key is to reach out for help. Making the call, sending the email, and being humble enough to admit that you can't do this on your own are the first steps. They're big steps for many leaders, but they're essential.

The second thing that you need to know about being stuck is that it will require a big move on your part. You can't get unstuck merely by making some tweaks or a few minor adjustments. I couldn't have gotten my car out of the ditch by detaching my rear-view mirror and carrying it out with me. No, you get unstuck by making big, bold moves, and that calls for courage. Courage seems to be a theme throughout these principles, does it not? Be willing

YOUR HELP WILL COME FROM SOMEBODY ON THE OUTSIDE.

to ask for help, and be willing to make big moves in response to the help you receive. That's how you get out of the ditch.

If you're feeling stuck, keep these two things in mind. Number one, you're going to get unstuck thanks to help from the outside. Think outside the box as to who it might be who can best help you. And number two, you're going to get unstuck only if you have the courage to make that bold move.

You don't have to stay stuck. You can move forward with a little bit of courage.

YOU'RE GOING TO GET UNSTUCK THANKS TO HELP FROM THE OUTSIDE. THINK OUTSIDE THE BOX AS TO WHO IT MIGHT BE WHO CAN BEST HELP YOU.

32

WHAT'S IMPORTANT

POWER POINT THIRTY-TWO

TURBO LEADERSHIP

156

Every leader must define what's important to him or her. If *everything* is important to you, then nothing is important to you. Not truly. You have to know. I have friends who are very successful in leading their organizations, but they've lost their families. Some have widened their spheres of influence, but on the inside, they are dying and withering away. Others, on the outside, seem to be fulfilled, but their satisfaction level is very low. Do you know why? Because they did not define what was important to them.

For example, if you value your family, then you're going to prioritize them. In fact, your actions will show you and others what's important to you. You'll spend time with your family and have a vision for your future as a family. You'll leave the office when you say you're going to leave the office and protect your boundaries when you're not at work by turning off your computer and your phone. You'll prioritize family because that's truly important to you. You can say that people are important to you, but if you don't show it through your actions—if you're never around people but consider them an intrusion, an interruption—others are going to be able to tell.

People will have these meetings in the hallway outside your office, whispering, "Should we talk to her today?" "Should we talk to him today?" Maybe they hesitate to come in and actually speak to you. Maybe they won't meet your eyes in meetings and only email you as a last resort. You can keep telling people that your door is always open—that they can come to you anytime—but if your behavior tells a different story, they're not going to feel safe approaching and confiding in you. You're going to build a company culture of fear and intimidation. This is just one example of the negative effect it can have when you don't identify and live out what's truly important. Define what you value. Then, make sure that your definition and your actions are congruent.

> **DEFINE WHAT YOU VALUE. THEN, MAKE SURE THAT YOUR DEFINITION AND YOUR ACTIONS ARE CONGRUENT.**

Start here: What are the top five most significant things in your life? Make a list. Rank them. Be honest with yourself about where you are today—not necessarily where you want to be. If you don't identify these five, the rest of the secondary priorities and cares of life are going to run over the important things, and the tyranny of the urgent is going to destroy what's important in your life. Make a list of what you cherish, and lean into those things. Come up with an action plan to truly prioritize them, and make sure your actions match your words.

LEADING WHERE YOU HAVEN'T BEEN

Despite many voices that claim the contrary, it is possible as leaders to take people where we haven't been. You *can* take people where you haven't gone before. Every large company was a small company at one time. Every successful CEO was once a person who started with little experience. Every large church used to be a small church. Every large church pastor used to be a small church pastor—or even a church planter. The truth is that each and every one of us has taken people where we have never gone. Therefore, you can be vulnerable about it and not pretend with your people. Don't be a leader who claims to always know where you're going.

The Bible holds a great example of what self-aware leadership should look like. In the Old Testament, Joshua turned to his people and said, "Hey guys, we have not come this way before. This is new for me, and it's new for you. Let's go do this thing together." I think Joshua was smart. What a great outlook he had! He could have said something along the lines of, "Well, I think I know what I'm doing. Just follow me. Don't ask a whole lot of questions." Sound like any leaders you've encountered in your own journey? Yeah, me too. The problem here is that people can see through this veneer. They know you haven't been where you're going; neither have they. Instead of inspiring confidence, this kind of self-important attitude—this unhealthy ego—detracts from your plausibility. They begin to see you as someone who will promote yourself even at their expense.

Vulnerable, authentic, genuine leaders put it all out there in the open. They're up-front with their teams about the fact that they're in uncharted territory—no one on the team has done it in the exact way they're pursuing it today. These leaders share the message that, though they may not have instituted that program... raised this much money... built that building... launched a new product... or cultivated a space for the business to grow—they're willing to give it a shot. With their team working together, they'll achieve the desired outcome.

YOU CAN TAKE PEOPLE WHERE YOU HAVEN'T GONE BEFORE.

Here is the attitude to have when you find yourself leading your people somewhere new: "I think we can. Do you think we can? Well, that's all we need to know. If all of us think we can, let's go make it happen." Find out who on your team has skills and experience, siphon help from outside your team, and find the resources and materials you need that you don't have yet. Be straightforward about the fact that this is new territory, and you'll inspire confidence in those you're leading. It's that simple. You will *always* lead people where you have never been before. So own up to that fact, and go. Lead the people.

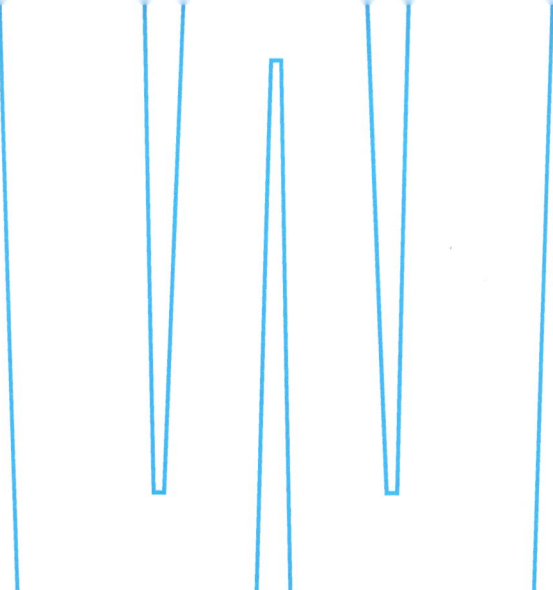

What is the most difficult decision you as a leader can make? What decision, if not made, is going to stymie your leadership and bog you down in stagnation? It's not something we'd automatically identify as a roadblock for leaders because it doesn't appear on evaluations, get revealed in data sets, or come up in board meetings. Yet, it has tripped up many leaders over the years.

It's simply this: Too many people don't understand forgiveness. They don't make the decision to forgive and move on. Forgive and move on.

First, let's be honest: People have done you wrong. They've disappointed you, said one thing and done another thing, and betrayed you. You've gone through tough times, been hurt, and have had to walk away from some relationships because of people's unwillingness to show you respect and decency. Here's the thing: As a leader, if you're not bleeding, you're not leading. I write about that in my book *Leadership Pain*. It's a difficult principle to absorb, but if you take a look at your past, you'll see that your journey is littered with these moments.

That's just part of life. The real question is not, "Did you get hurt?" or "Did people do you wrong?" The real question is this:

"How have you *responded* to it?" This is why your leadership can be thwarted by your answer. If you haven't integrated grace into your life, forgiven them, and moved on, these people are living rent-free in your head. The memories of their faults and the emotions, thoughts, and pain you experienced, as a result, will replay in your mind—even when you want them to stop. These people occupy space in your head and exert control over your life, and it's not because *they* broke, entered, and are squatting. It is because *you* are allowing them to live there. We have control over what we hold onto, and as hard as it may be to let it go, we have the power to forgive and move on.

AS A LEADER, IF YOU'RE NOT BLEEDING, YOU'RE NOT LEADING. IF YOU TAKE A LOOK AT YOUR PAST, YOU'LL SEE THAT YOUR JOURNEY IS LITTERED WITH THESE MOMENTS.

So, here's my challenge for you. Whom do you need to forgive? Your list may be short, but allow me to lengthen it a little bit. These people don't have to ask for forgiveness to be forgiven. You need to evict that from your mind. Get rid of that mindset, and decide to forgive—no matter what. This is imperative to moving forward effectively because once your brain is clear, your heart will also be able to clear itself and not be muddled with regrets and bitterness. You'll let the grudges go because you'll understand that holding onto them is like drinking poison and expecting the other person to die. Don't do that anymore. Forgive, and move on. You will be a healthier leader. Let it go.

(THEY DON'T) HAVE TO ASK FOR FORGIVENESS

POWER POINT THIRTY-FIVE

35 /// SELLING YOUR IDEA

TURBO LEADERSHIP

170

SELLING YOUR IDEA

If you are a leader, you have ideas. And if you are a leader, you're going to try to convince others about how great your ideas are. That's what leaders do. They get an idea, tell others about it, build a coalition or alliance, and then make plans to implement that concept. The question is, *How do I even get out of the gate? How do I sell my idea?* Here's a simple thought: Do not sell the *thing*; sell the *benefit* of the thing.

I do a lot of public speaking, and I always wear a microphone. I did not necessarily buy the microphone. I bought the advantage of an amplified voice. I wear a shirt every day. I did not buy a shirt. I bought the blessing of warmth, modesty, and comfort. I wear a watch because of its constant assistance in telling time. Starting to get the idea?

You purchase a vacuum cleaner, for example. But really, in essence, you did not buy a vacuum cleaner. You didn't purchase it in order to leave it in the box and stare at it in the corner of the room. You bought the *benefit* of a vacuum cleaner—cleanliness and a lack of dust or pet hair. Nobody buys *stuff*. They buy that stuff's usefulness. Oftentimes, when we start with the product, we lose people quickly because they've been pitched an endless array of goods. Through television, radio, social media, door-to-door salesmen, and the stores they visit, they're inundated with products they could spend money on. However, when you start first by talking to people about the assets of the product you're selling, it opens their minds to possibilities before they shut down. You had an idea, and you saw possibilities, but the thing that you have to sell to your customers and clients are the benefits.

An estate attorney sells wills and estates not because people value pieces of paper but because they value leaving their family and loved ones with security. Real estate agents sell property not because the properties in themselves are inherently valuable but because buyers see the potential to build a business or a life on that property. A church "sells" its mission and vision not because people think the church building is so important but because its

DO NOT SELL THE THING: SELL THE BENEFIT OF THE THING.

values and ideals are things that Christians (and sometimes even non-Christians) can get behind.

So the next time you're going into a meeting, or you're talking about an idea, don't sell the thing. Sell the benefits. Here's a little homework for you: Make a list of all the advantages—the most valuable perks—that come with it. Then, you can take those benefits into the meeting so that people can buy into them, see the possibilities, and say yes to your idea.

POWER POINT THIRTY-SIX

TURBO LEADERSHIP

174

/// DECISION-MAKING VS. IMPLEMENTATION

I want to save you some frustration on your leadership journey. Oftentimes, many of us get stuck between making decisions and seeing them come to pass. Here's how we fix that: Bridge the gap between decision-making and implementation. Think you're already implementing an idea? Just meeting with your group or your team and making a decision does not mean it's going to get done. Unfortunately, I get calls from organizations all the time saying, "Well, we had a meeting, conducted feasibility studies, and went through the whole process. We hired a consultant, brought in coaches, and decided the best way to do this . . . but it did not happen."

This unfortunate scenario occurs frequently in businesses, churches, and even families because we confuse decision-making with implementation. Making the decision is essential, it's true, but that's the primary step. It's setting an intention as we talked about earlier. It's resolving to do something. Implementation, on the other hand, is the process of moving the decided-upon idea from concept to reality. It's when you hit the ground running. It's the hours of work and energy that go into actually making the thing happen. There has to be a connection between the two, or else we'll never move into the implementation phase.

This is why so many people never complete what our culture has come to call New Year's resolutions. They've made decisions to move towards something, but they never put those decisions into practice. This is often because there's no concrete plan by which to do so. We handicap ourselves severely by making vague decisions with no roadmap to get us to our destinations and then wonder why we never arrive. Let's not do that any longer. Let's have a plan.

Here's a practical example: Imagine that you're leaving your house to go to a certain destination. At home, the decision was made regarding where to go. However, at the point you leave your house, you have to coordinate a route to get you from your location to the

BRIDGE THE GAP BETWEEN DECISION—MAKING AND IMPLEMENTATION.

desired place. Steps should show your progress the entire way to make sure that your implementation is successful. Do not confuse these two principles, or you could end up lost on the side of the road on the way to your goals. Make a plan, stick to it, and you'll find that it's been implemented before you know it.

Next time you make a decision, ensure that you have an implementation plan to go with it. Seek counsel from experienced people who can give you feedback. Find those who have been there before—those you can learn from and who can mentor you. Then, show up, and do the work, guided by your mentors and driven by your decision. Only when you combine decision-making and implementation will you get to your destination and begin achieving those goals.

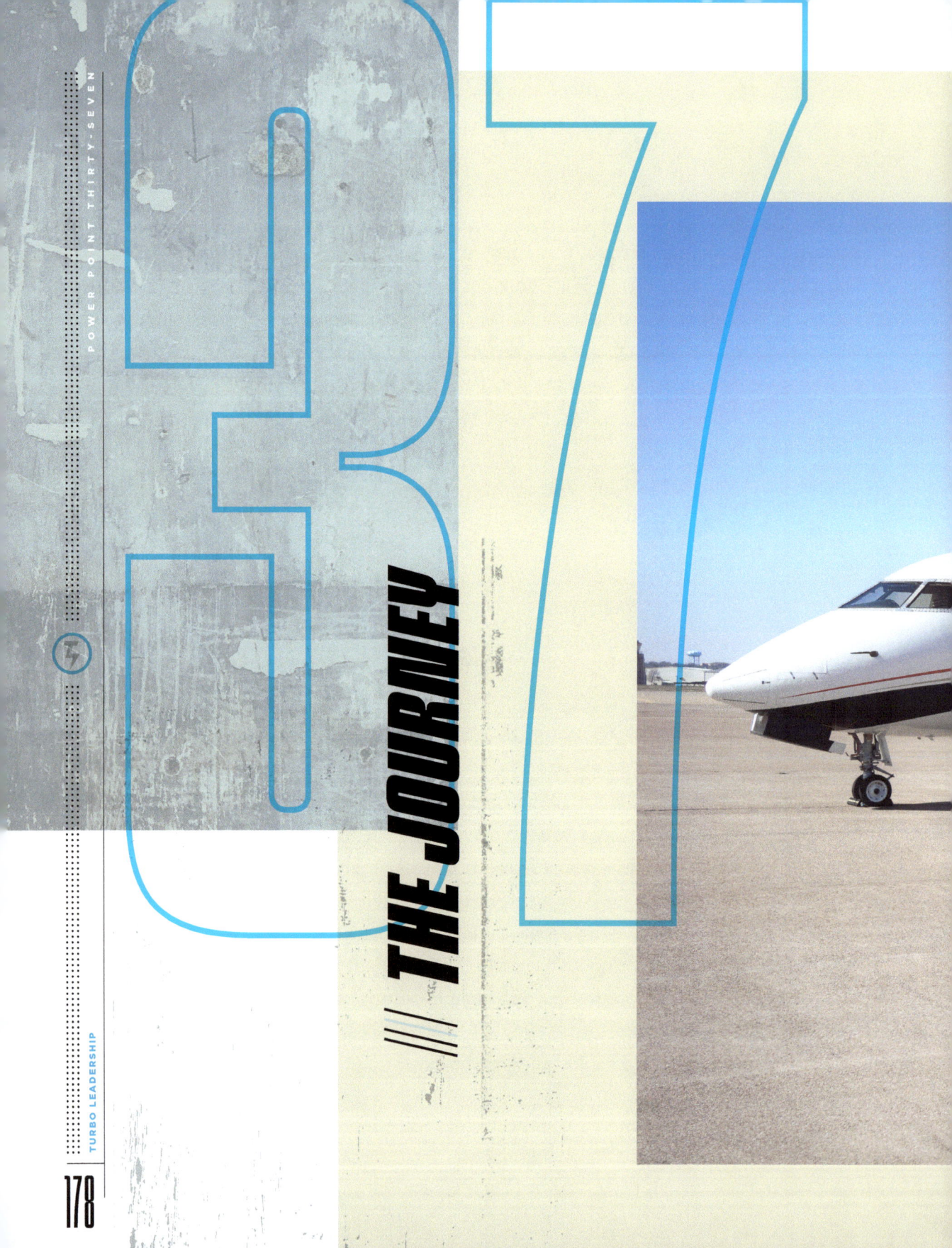

POWER POINT THIRTY-SEVEN

37
THE JOURNEY

TURBO LEADERSHIP

178

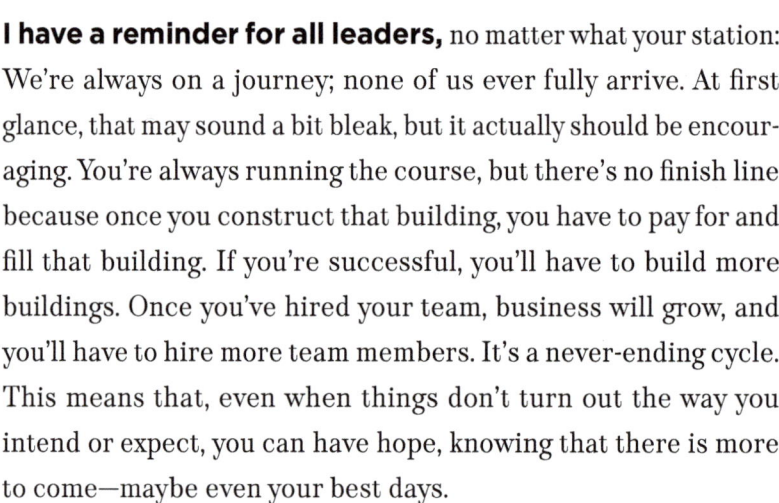

I have a reminder for all leaders, no matter what your station: We're always on a journey; none of us ever fully arrive. At first glance, that may sound a bit bleak, but it actually should be encouraging. You're always running the course, but there's no finish line because once you construct that building, you have to pay for and fill that building. If you're successful, you'll have to build more buildings. Once you've hired your team, business will grow, and you'll have to hire more team members. It's a never-ending cycle. This means that, even when things don't turn out the way you intend or expect, you can have hope, knowing that there is more to come—maybe even your best days.

You are always on a journey, never arriving. The mindset that goes with that is, *I'm okay with being on a journey*. If you're looking for a point of arrival or a specific destination, you won't get there. Instead of being grateful for what has been and excited for what is to come, you'll be chronically dissatisfied and frustrated when your finish line morphs into another starting line. It's a little bit like waiting for your GPS to say, "Your final destination is on the right." That always feels good, doesn't it? But there's no such thing as a final destination in leadership.

Pastors: What is your point of arrival—people getting saved? If you have a hundred people saved next Sunday, is that an arrival? No, you will then aim for two hundred. Businessmen and women: You made $10 million yesterday. Are you happy with that, in the sense that you will never aim for anything else? Have you arrived? Can you retire and never set another goal? No! You're on the journey. You're looking ahead to the next thing, making plans and thanking people for contributing to how far you've come today while enlisting their aid to get you where you're headed tomorrow. You're thinking, *If I made ten million yesterday, I could make a hundred million by the end of the week.* I'm not against that. That's healthy. That's part of the role of a leader, after all—to chart the uncharted waters and keep pressing into new territory.

SET A CULTURE THAT CREATES AN EXPECTATION THAT WE ARE IN THIS TOGETHER FOR THE LONG HAUL.

If you as a leader are looking at leading your people to the point of arrival—a GPS coordinate, a destination—and you keep making those kinds of speeches, setting those kinds of expectations, and using that kind of language with your people, they will also forget that they are on a journey. Set a culture that creates an expectation that we are in this together for the long haul. Celebrate wins and milestones, absolutely, but keep in mind that you are on a journey, never arriving. Take your people with you, honor the steps along the way, but keep saying to yourself, *I'm on a journey with no point of arrival.* When you get down to it, that is exciting.

YOU ARE ALWAYS ON A JOURNEY, NEVER ARRIVING.

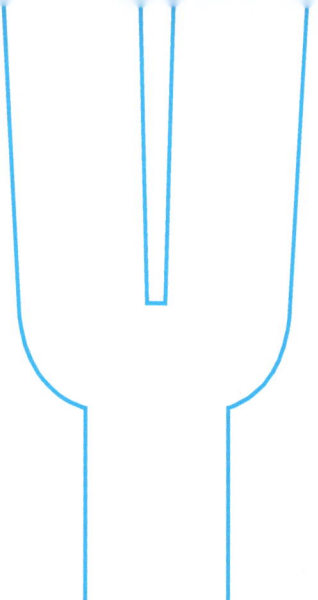

Your life is full of purpose.

All of us have purpose. It looks different for each one of us, depending on what our callings, gifts, and talents are. It depends where we live, what our situation is, who the people that we know are, and what we've been called upon to do or be.

Your purpose might be to encourage somebody, to be the CEO of a company, or to raise good kids in your home as a homemaker. Your purpose might be to be a financial wizard. An inventor. An educator. An astronaut. A lawyer. An economist. An artist. A nurse. An engineer. A social worker. A zookeeper. A scientist. A chef. A teacher. An investor. A pastor. Any number of purposes can emerge for your life.

Here's another beautiful thing: we can each have multiple purposes throughout our individual lives. While one decade of your life may be devoted to business, the next is devoted to childrearing. One season may be for building your personal brand; the next may be seeking out proteges to mentor as they're doing the same. One year may see you navigating marriage while the next may bring a dive into parenthood. No matter what your purpose is in any given season, the purpose you're walking in right now has to do with the people around you.

Your purpose attracts your people. I create leadership content to influence influencers. That's my purpose. And as soon as I got clear about that, people started coming into my life. They are the people who coach me and the people I coach. They are the leaders I need to learn from and the leaders who are learning from me. They are influencers who need help and influencers who have help to offer to me in return. Sometimes, these two groups overlap, as well! It's a beautiful thing to see, and we need to recognize it when it starts happening. If not, we'll miss some of these key relationships because we won't be looking for them. Who knows how many chances to meet wonderful people and do amazing things together each of us has forfeited simply because we weren't aware of those in our lives?

As soon as you get clear about your purpose, people will start appearing. And when people appear, they are providential in your life. Be thankful for, embrace, and learn from them. Make the most of these relationships. You may not understand everything about why certain people are emerging in your life, but keep reminding yourself: *My purpose attracts the right people.* Then, go out, and form bonds with them. They very well might be lifelong friends and partners!

> **NO MATTER WHAT YOUR PURPOSE IS IN ANY GIVEN SEASON, THE PURPOSE YOU'RE WALKING IN RIGHT NOW HAS TO DO WITH THE PEOPLE AROUND YOU.**

39 // CHOICE-RICH

POWER POINT THIRTY-NINE

TURBO LEADERSHIP

190

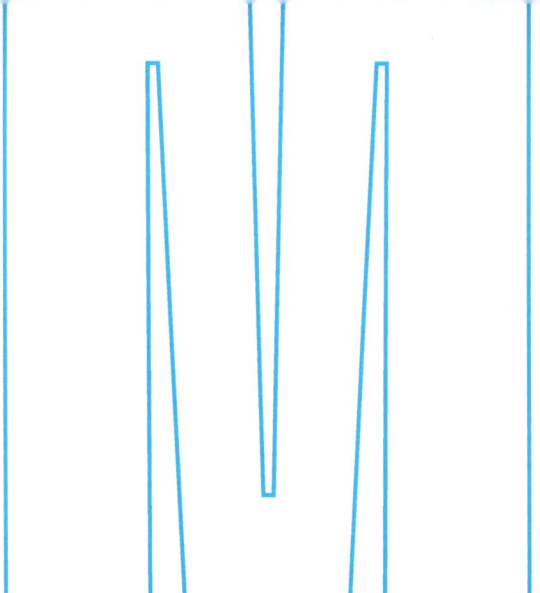

Maybe some (or all) of the following thoughts have run through your head today:

I don't have enough time.

I'm too busy.

I can't get it all done.

I'm completely overwhelmed!

Maybe I should just throw in the towel.

Do these feelings have anything to do with time management? My answer to that question is no.

I don't believe that there's any such thing as time management, and here's why: You can only manage that which you create, and you don't create time. You can't control it. You can't stop it. You can't rewind it, and so you cannot manage it. Managing time is like raking water. You're moving it around, but you're not managing anything. It's going to obey its natural laws regardless of how much you wish it would bend to your will.

Instead of saying, "I am time-poor," I want you to think about the concept of being choice-rich. This is a paradigm shift for all of us. You are not time-poor. You are choice-rich. In fact, it is precisely because you have so many options that you feel like you're time-poor. However, if you focus on your choices and making good ones—healthy choices, choices that will allow you to move ahead in the direction you want to go in—then something in your mindset will shift. Instead of automatically thinking, *I don't have enough time,* you're going to be able to flip the script and make a new default thinking pattern for yourself: *I have a lot of choices. I am in control of which one I select.*

Do you see what happens in your brain when you say that to yourself? When you say, *I don't have enough time,* it takes you down. You get discouraged. Everything feels like it's overwhelming. You feel inadequate. You're not able to appreciate where you are because you're only focused on what hasn't been done yet. Conversely, when you say, *I have a lot of choices,* it takes you up! You feel happier, more grateful, and more empowered. You remind yourself of the agency you possess over what you can control.

One is an upper. One is a downer. Stop saying, "I don't have enough time." You are not time-poor. Keep reminding yourself of this truth. You only feel that way because you're choice-rich. Once we realize this, it will become infinitely easier to turn stressful days into thankful days and apparent setbacks into opportunities that propel us forward in life.

Know your options. Select one from among the many. Don't focus on being time-poor; focus on the choice you have the power to make right now, today. If you'll do that, your choices, which are consequential, will lead you to achieving the goals you have set for your life.

> **MANAGING TIME IS LIKE RAKING WATER. YOU'RE MOVING IT AROUND, BUT YOU'RE NOT MANAGING ANYTHING.**

40

POWER POINT FORTY

TURBO LEADERSHIP

194

MY GREATEST REGRET

MY GREATEST REGRET

195

Perhaps you've heard these questions in your leadership journey before:

"What's your greatest regret?"

"If you could say something to your younger self, what would that be?"

"If you had a do-over, what would you do over?"

These are all the same question asked in different ways. I receive endless variations of these questions as I travel across the world, and I want to share my answer with you as I have given this quite a bit of personal thought.

The greatest regret that I have in my leadership journey is that I did not have coaches and mentors in my life. I didn't have anyone who could see something in me, take an interest in me—not for their own sake or for what I could do for them. No one put their arm around me and said, "Sam, I see something in you. Let me help you, so you don't have to make the same mistakes that I have made. Let me fast-track your journey." I could be in a completely different place today if someone had said this to me years ago. I could have identified some of my weaknesses, strengths, flaws, and blind spots if someone had taken me under their wing and shown me how to do leadership as a younger man.

I was born and raised in a pastor's home in India. I have gone to Bible college and been a youth pastor, a senior pastor, and even a college university president. I write books. I talk to people who are leaders . . . and sadly, I don't recall anyone in my life ever saying to me, "Sam, I see something in you. Let me save you from yourself. Sam, let me help you." But neither did I have the bandwidth to even think that I could ask for help.

If we're going to build a legacy of mentorship and coaching for the generation to come after us, we have to be willing to seek out mentors of our own. We have to start the culture of learning from those a few steps ahead of us. We have to shift the narrative today. It's not enough to assent to the fact that coaches are beneficial,

THE GREATEST REGRET THAT I HAVE IN MY LEADERSHIP JOURNEY IS THAT I DID NOT HAVE COACHES AND MENTORS IN MY LIFE.

that we need others' wisdom. We have to do the work of actually putting this principle into practice. That's the only way things will change. That's the only way our legacies, our leadership, and our lives will change.

My life would be much different if I'd had mentors and coaches in my life. Your destiny can change forever if you will get some mentors and coaches in *your* life. Don't wait—you're not getting any younger. Reaching out to a coach or mentor could be a life-changer for you.

PHOTO CREDITS

Altansukh E, 87
Andrew van Tilborgh, 9, 13, 17, 21, 25, 31, 35, 43, 45, 46, 53, 57, 59, 67, 75, 79, 83, 96, 99, 101, 102, 105, 115, 121, 129, 145, 151, 161, 171, 175, 179, 189, 195
Arturo Castaneyra, 109
Brooke Cagle, 91
C7ear7ove7, 119
Clay Banks, 49
Dan Cristian, 191
Denys Nevozhai, 148
Donny Jiang, 155
Dustin Tramel, 169
Emile Seguin, 19
Fabien Bazanegue, 95
Fabio Comparelli, 125
Florin Bica, 139
Jack Cross, 182
Jack Sloop, 147
Jeremy Beadle, 136
Jessica Rockowitz, 157
Jon Tyson, 29
Kyle Glenn, 93
Mariano Werneck, 1, 2, 6, 7, 200
Marissa Grootes, 135
Matteo Vistocco, 39
Rostyslav Savchyn, 165
Scott Rodgerson, 3, 5, 199
Stormseeker, 143
Susan Q Yin, 131
Sydney Rae, All Pages
Tyler Harris, 133
Zach Camp, 113

POWER POINTS FOR MAXIMUM PERFORMANCE